TREES OF
the Northern Pacific Coast

HELP US KEEP THIS GUIDE UP TO DATE

Every effort has been made by the author and editors to make this guide as accurate and useful as possible. However, many things can change after a guide is published—regulations change, facilities come under new management, and so forth.

We would love to hear from you concerning your experiences with this guide and how you feel it could be improved and kept up to date. While we may not be able to respond to all comments and suggestions, we'll take them to heart, and we'll also make certain to share them with the author. Please send your comments and suggestions to falconeditorial@rowman.com.

Thank you for your input!

TREES OF
the Northern
Pacific Coast

Identifying the Region's Prominent Trees

Robert Weiss

ESSEX, CONNECTICUT

An imprint of Globe Pequot, the trade division of
The Rowman & Littlefield Publishing Group, Inc.
4501 Forbes Blvd., Ste. 200
Lanham, MD 20706
www.rowman.com

Falcon and FalconGuides are registered trademarks and Make Adventure Your Story is a
trademark of The Rowman & Littlefield Publishing Group, Inc.

Distributed by NATIONAL BOOK NETWORK

Copyright © 2024 by The Rowman & Littlefield Publishing Group, Inc.
Photos by Robert Weiss unless otherwise noted
Maps by Melissa Baker and The Rowman & Littlefield Publishing Group, Inc.

British Library Cataloguing in Publication Information available

Library of Congress Cataloging-in-Publication Data
Names: Weiss, Robert (Botanist), author.
Title: Trees of the Northern Pacific Coast : identifying the region's prominent trees /
  Robert Weiss.
Other titles: Falcon guide
Description: Essex, Connecticut : FalconGuides, [2024] | Series: Falcon Guides | Includes
  bibliographical references. | Summary: "Trees of the Northern Pacific Coast is a photographic
  guidebook that identifies over sixty of the most prominent native and naturalized tree species
  of the coastal region spanning from California, Oregon, and Washington, to British Columbia
  and Southern Alaska"— Provided by publisher.
Identifiers: LCCN 2023040275 (print) | LCCN 2023040276 (ebook) | ISBN 9781493080021
  (paperback) | ISBN 9781493080038 (epub)
Subjects: LCSH: Trees—Northwest, Pacific—Identification. | Forests and forestry—Northwest,
  Pacific. | Guidebooks.
Classification: LCC QK144 .W45 2024 (print) | LCC QK144 (ebook) | DDC 582.16—dc23/
  eng/20231201
LC record available at https://lccn.loc.gov/2023040275
LC ebook record available at https://lccn.loc.gov/2023040276

♾™ The paper used in this publication meets the minimum requirements of American National
Standard for Information Sciences—Permanence of Paper for Printed Library Materials, ANSI/
NISO Z39.48-1992.

The authors and The Rowman & Littlefield Publishing Group, Inc., assume
no liability for accidents happening to, or injuries sustained by, readers who
engage in the activities described in this book.

CONTENTS

ACKNOWLEDGMENTS

I would like to thank the following people for their help in reviewing this book and supplying additional photos: Amanda Grady, Christopher Lee, Ed C. Jenson, Joelene Tamm, Kim Corella, Lorraine Maclauchlan PhD, Monica Gaylord, Nicholas Wilhelmi, Robert L. Edmonds, Tom Smith, Walter Fertig, William C. Woodruff, and Anna Webb.

PACIFIC
OCEAN

ATLANTIC
OCEAN

Alaska

Yukon

Northwest
Territory

Nunavit

Baffin
Island

British
Columbia

Alberta

Saskatchewan

Manitoba

Ontario

Quebec

Newfoundland

Washington

Montana

North
Dakota

Minnesota

New
Brunswick

Nova Scotia

Oregon

Idaho

Maine

New Hampshire
Vermont
Massachusetts
Rhode Island
Connecticut

Wyoming

South
Dakota

Wisconsin

Michigan

New York

Pennsylvania

Nevada

Nebraska

Iowa

New Jersey
Delaware
Maryland

Utah

Colorado

Illinois

Indiana

Ohio

West
Virginia

Virginia

California

Kansas

Missouri

Kentucky

Arizona

New
Mexico

Oklahoma

Tennessee

North Carolina

Arkansas

South
Carolina

Texas

Mississippi

Alabama

Georgia

Louisiana

Florida

INTRODUCTION

This manual covers identification and basic hazard considerations of the Pacific coast trees, which includes southern and southeastern Alaska, British Columbia (mainly west of the Rocky Mountains and south of the northern boreal forest), Washington, Oregon, and California. It also includes western Nevada along the California border, which includes the Sierra Nevada and White Mountains areas. The trees selected for this manual are tall enough at maturity to contact electric power lines or cause damage to objects below when falling, like in campgrounds. Most of the trees discussed in detail are native—however, a few are introduced trees that have become naturalized. Native trees with limited distribution, with short stature, or that occur primarily in remote locations geographically are not described in detail in this manual. Several native ranges of the cypresses are in more remote locations mainly away from paved roads or public structures, so they were incorporated into a general description under Monterey cypress. Willows are grouped together under Goodding willow, since there are similar features among species within the genus and the trees can be hard to identify in thick riparian vegetation. Whitebark pine is not a tall tree but is included with a species description due to its widespread range and ecological interest. As of December 2022, whitebark pine has been listed as threatened under the Endangered Species Act by the US Fish and Wildlife Service.

Descriptions of species or grouping of species generally include the native or invasive range, botanical description (i.e., height, leaves, fruit), plant communities and associated species, similar species and identifying characteristics, biotic and abiotic issues (not all inclusive), range map, and photos. The botanical descriptions are normally for trees growing in their home range. "Similar trees" describes other trees in their native ranges and occasionally non-native trees. The biotic and abiotic issues that are discussed are normally those that cause mortality or live tree failure of mature trees in this manual, and it is only a partial listing of factors and somewhat of a basic or beginner guide to these types of issues. The summer and winter taxonomic keys list only those trees mentioned in this manual and do not include all the shorter native trees present on the Pacific coast. The photos try to depict each tree in a natural setting and with identifying characteristics of the species.

This manual is designed for persons in the arboriculture trade, government agencies, and the general public. The taxonomy tries to follow Flora of North America (eFloras.org).

IDENTIFYING TREES

Tree definition and anatomy. A tree is a woody perennial plant that usually consists of a single stem (some may have multiple stems, like tree of heaven). Some publications say the definition of a tree is that the height at maturity should be at least 3.5 m (15 feet) or taller. Most species of woody shrubs with multiple stems are less than 3.5 meters tall. Some exceptions include several manzanita and ceanothus species and red shank (*Adenostoma sparsifolium*). The compounds (including lignin and cellulose) inside the stem and branches make it hard and rigid, which in turn makes tall mature trees heavy and potentially hazardous when they fall. Trees have a vascular cambium running up and down the stem, which includes the xylem and the phloem. If abiotic or biotic factors affect the processes of the xylem or phloem, the tree can alter its growth or potentially die. Leaf-defoliating insects can affect photosynthesis in the leaves, which alters the flow of carbohydrates in the phloem. Root rot diseases mainly affect the roots, which alter water and nutrient flow in the xylem. Bark beetles can girdle a cambium, which can affect both the xylem and the phloem. Herbicides can be applied as a broadcast or contact spray affecting the leaves and photosynthesis and as a pre-emergence affecting the plants through the roots.

Tree scents. Some of the conifers and hardwoods in this manual have characteristic scents when the leaves or needles are rubbed or crushed. Some trees can be smelled from a distance before even seeing them. This characteristic helps identify trees at any age as long as the live needles or leaves can be reached. *Abies* is a genus in particular where the needles in nearly every species have a distinct scent. Grand fir (white fir is similar but milder), Pacific silver fir, noble fir (red fir is similar), subalpine fir, and also Douglas fir all have distinctive scents in the needles. Other conifers with needle or leaf scents include mountain and western hemlock, spruces, incense cedar, western red cedar, Alaska yellow cedar, Port Orford cedar, cypresses, junipers, California bay, tree of heaven, and *Eucalyptus* spp. Seedlings from these species that are less than a meter tall can be identified by their scents.

Winter identification. This mainly applies to hardwoods. Only one native conifer on the West Coast is deciduous. Larix is relatively easy to identify in the winter months since it has a characteristic conical crown like most other conifers. Oaks can be identified in the winter by the presence of several buds on the ends of twigs and branches. Alders can be identified by the small conelike fruits and mostly stalked buds. The winter buds of black cottonwood, plains cottonwood, and Fremont cottonwood have resins and scents useful for identifying them versus willows and other trees in the winter months. Willows only have one scale on their winter buds, compared to two-plus scales for many other genuses.

Some species, like black locust, have thorns on the stems. Opposite or alternate branching can be used in the winter months to help distinguish a genus or species (e.g., opposite branches of maples or ashes compared with alternate branches from those of alders, cottonwoods, and oaks). Walnuts have chambered piths in the twigs that help identification. Winter buds and leaf scars can often aid, combined with other characteristics, in identifying hardwoods to genus.

Chambered twig pith of walnut

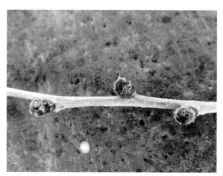

Siberian elm buds with hairy scale margins

Single-scaled buds of willow

Stalked buds of red alder

Large leaf scar and hairy bud of tree of heaven

Winter buds of black oak

Bark. Bark can be a useful characteristic to identify trees any time of year. Bark texture and color can vary greatly from young versus mature trees in the same species. Some species, like Pacific madrone and eucalyptus, shed the outer bark, leaving an inner bark exposed that aids identification of those particular species or genuses. Sitka spruce and mountainous lodgepole pine have scaly bark. Redwood and giant sequoia have orange-brown, very thick, fibrous bark. Photos for the individual species descriptions are usually of bark on mature trees.

Bark of young noble fir before full maturity   Bark of birch trees before turning white and peeling

Leaves and needles. These are very useful for identification and may be the best characteristic for identifying most trees. Hardwoods can have leaf margins that are entire, serrated, crenate, toothed, spine-toothed, or lobed, and the leaf edges can be plane or wavy. Leaf shapes can be linear, oblong, lanceolate, oblanceolate, ovate, cordate, or round. Leaves are usually singly attached to the stem, or are compound (pinnate, palmate). Some hardwood leaves are evergreen, some deciduous, and a few semi-deciduous. Leaf surfaces can be glabrous, glaucous, or hairy. Conifers can have scales, individual needles, needles in fascicles (bundles) that are wrapped in a sheath (e.g., genus Pinus), or clustered as in larches. Conifer needles can be blunt tipped, pointed, or spine tipped. Many conifers have needles or scales with lines of white stomata. Describing patterns of white stomata are used for species when it significantly aids in identification. Most conifers and several hardwoods have evergreen needles or leaves, which can be used year-round for identification.

Alternate branching of elm

Compound leaf of walnut with serrated leaflet margins

Doubly serrate leaf margins of alder leaves

Opposite compound leaves of ash

Palmate leaves and spiny capsule of invasive horse chestnut tree

Clustered needles of larch

Crenate leaf margin of cordate-shaped cottonwood leaves

Lobed leaf margins of maple leaves

Palm leaf frond with palmate lobing

Pinyon (*Pinus*) needles in fascicles of two to five

Serrate leaf margins of birch leaves

Spine-tipped needles of bristlecone fir

Spine-toothed leaf margins of an oak

Wavy leaf margins of Pacific wax myrtle

Female cones and fruiting structures can be very important in identification when they are present. Many trees, like conifers and oaks, usually drop their cones or fruit on the ground, which can aid in determining species several years after they fell. The genus *Abies* and whitebark pine are examples of trees that have cones that disintegrate while on the tree. Pinaceae have cones with non-peltate scales, while most Cupressaceae have cones with peltate scales. Oaks and tan oak

Scaled leaves and cones with peltate scales of a cypress

Legume fruit of a locust tree

have an acorn and attached cap, which is unique for western trees. Willow identification can be aided by using male (anther characteristics) or female (capsule characteristics) catkins. The flowers of some of the hardwood trees in this book are mentioned, especially if they aid in identification.

Samara fruit of silver maple with uneven winged seeds

Dead and fire-burned tree identification. If the dead leaves or needles are still on the tree, it can be identified fairly readily by comparing to similar live trees in the area. Conifers usually have a conical and symmetric shape to them, with a straight stem, also referred to as excurrent. Hardwoods usually have a rounded or spreading crown that is symmetric or asymmetric and stems slightly angled, also referred to as decurrent. There are exceptions for both. If the leaves and needles have dropped from the tree, they can possibly still be observed on the ground, along with fruits or cones. Also, observe the bark characteristics. When a tree has been dead for a few years, the bark characteristics start changing as it slowly decomposes. If a tree has been lightly burned by fire on the stem and crown, observe the bark characteristics and shape of the crown and branches. If the bark has been burned completely off the tree, I look at the general architecture of the tree (i.e., straight or leaning, single or multiple stemmed, conical or spreading tree shape), elevation of the site, and surrounding plant community.

FOREST TYPES

The forest types chosen are somewhat similar and somewhat based on the USA National Atlas major forest types and potential natural vegetation and Ecosystems of British Columbia. These types were chosen based on geography and the differences in species composition among them. They do not include all the forest types that occur along the Pacific Coast (i.e., some of the closed-cone and serpentine tree types), and many forest types were grouped together here. They can be referred to as zones or forests also. South-central Alaska has a mix of conifers and hardwoods, while southeastern Alaska has more conifers. British Columbia has more conifers in the coastal areas, while the interior areas can be mainly conifers or a mix of conifers and hardwoods. Washington and most of Oregon are dominated by conifers, with deciduous hardwoods occurring more often in riparian areas. Southwest Oregon and California have a mix of conifers, evergreen hardwoods, and deciduous hardwoods. Conifers dominate the higher elevations in California, with deciduous hardwoods being common in riparian areas. Evergreen hardwoods in California occur mainly at low to mid-elevations. Conifer diversity peaks where climates and tree ranges overlap. The highest diversity of conifers I have seen in small geographic areas are in the western Cascades from Mount Rainier in Washington south to Crater Lake in Oregon, and several areas of the Klamath-Siskiyou Mountains in northwestern California. Two areas in particular are Crystal Peak–Lake trail in Mount Rainier National Park, and Duck Lakes trail in the Russian Wilderness in northwestern California. Diversity of oak species can easily be found in central California near the coast, north and south of the San Francisco Bay area. Some of the areas where serpentine crosses with non-serpentine in mixed evergreen forest in the Klamath-Siskiyou Mountains have a high diversity of conifers and hardwoods in a very small area.

The **coastal type** includes species that are found growing along the Pacific Ocean and are influenced by coastal fogs. The main trees whose extensive ranges are centered along the coast include lodgepole pine or shore pine (*Pinus contorta* var. *contorta*), Sitka spruce, and bishop pine. Western red cedar, grand fir, western hemlock, red alder, redwood, and Pacific madrone (Puget Sound in Washington) are also coastal species. Torrey pine, Monterey cypress and Monterey pine, Gowen cypress, and Mendocino cypress have smaller, more restricted native habitats along the California coast. Sitka spruce, western hemlock, and lodgepole pine occur together from southeastern Alaska to the central California coast. Bishop pine and redwood are common along the northern and central California coastline. Pacific madrone is frequent along the Puget Sound in Washington. The coastal type is more extensive in southeastern Alaska where the numerous coastal islands occur and include Alaska yellow cedar and mountain hemlock. It is commonly referred to as the hemlock spruce type in coastal British Columbia and Alaska.

Douglas fir–hemlock–cedar. This type is dominant in western Washington and western Oregon at lower elevations. It also occurs on Vancouver Island and southwestern British Columbia. The main trees include western hemlock, Douglas fir, and western red cedar. Other trees include Pacific yew, grand fir, Pacific silver fir, noble fir, big-leaf maple, red alder, and black cottonwood. Alaska yellow cedar occurs in this type in British Columbia. Port Orford cedar occurs in southwestern Oregon. Sitka spruce occurs along coastal rivers reaching inland away from the coast. Due to Douglas fir being favored for regeneration after logging systems like clear-cuts, it is the dominant overstory tree in this region in the coast ranges and Cascades. Douglas fir var. *menziesii* is normally a seral species in this type. Western hemlock is the climax tree and is present in the overstory or under a canopy. Western red cedar is a climax tree in riparian areas and moister sites.

Douglas fir–grand fir. This type occurs mainly in central and eastern Oregon, parts of eastern Washington, and into Idaho. It is usually right above ponderosa pine forests. The main trees are Douglas fir and grand fir. Other common trees include western larch, ponderosa pine, lodgepole pine, and Engelmann spruce. In the east side of the southern Oregon Cascades, grand fir hybridizes with white fir. Incense cedar and sugar pine occur in this type in the central and southern Oregon Cascades.

Douglas fir type. This type occurs in north-central Washington and south-central British Columbia, flanked on the west by coastal forests and on the east by Rocky Mountain forests. This type is more extensive east in the Rocky Mountains. Douglas fir is the dominant conifer, at times in pure stands. Other trees occurring here include lodgepole pine, quaking aspen, paper birch, ponderosa pine, Engelmann spruce, and white spruce hybrids. This type also appears to be on dry sites west of the Cascade Mountains and into Northern California.

The **true fir type** is a mid-slope to lower subalpine area where many of the ski resort bases are located on the West Coast and usually has the highest diversity of conifers. It occurs above the Douglas fir–hemlock–cedar type in southwestern British Columbia, Washington, and northern Oregon, and above the mixed conifer type in southern Oregon and California. The main trees are Pacific silver fir, noble fir, white fir, and red fir (Shasta red fir). A climax community of Pacific silver fir grades into red fir from north to south. Pacific silver fir forests occur from the Canadian border to central Oregon. Pacific silver fir is less common of a forest type going north into British Columbia. Shasta red fir goes from central Oregon to the northern Sierra Nevada, where it is replaced by red fir through most of the length of the Sierra Nevada. Other trees include Alaska yellow cedar, mountain hemlock, Douglas fir, western hemlock, Jeffrey pine, lodgepole pine, quaking aspen, Brewer spruce (northwestern California),

True fir forest with noble fir

subalpine fir, and Engelmann spruce. This type has been referred to as Pacific silver fir and red fir types.

The **subalpine type** includes those areas right below the treeless alpine zone. It occupies the highest-elevation tree zone and is usually just above the true fir zone from Washington to California. In areas with cold air pockets or farther up north in British Columbia and Alaska, this type can be extensive, dropping down to much lower elevations than those that occur in California. Trees are shorter here than in the true fir type. The main trees are alpine larch, whitebark pine, foxtail pine, bristlecone pine (White Mountains of the California-Nevada border), subalpine fir, limber pine, mountain hemlock, lodgepole pine, Alaska yellow cedar, and Engelmann spruce. Pacific silver fir, red fir, and western larch reach into this type from lower elevations. Jeffrey pine and white fir can occur in this type in Southern California. Mountain hemlock forests occur from southern Alaska and British Columbia south to the central Sierra Nevada in California. Subalpine fir and Engelmann spruce stands are common on sites slightly east in the same mountain ranges of mountain hemlock stands from Canada to southern Oregon. Western white pine and lodgepole pine become more common in this type in the Sierra Nevada. Limber pine occurs in this type from the central Sierra Nevada to the mountains of Southern California. Elevations for this type decrease from south to north. A subalpine forest in Southern California can occur around 10,000 feet, while it drops to 500 feet (coastal Alaska) and 2,500 feet (interior British Columbia).

Subboreal white spruce-hardwood forest. This type occurs in the central part of British Columbia and south-central Alaska. White spruce and white spruce hybrids are the dominant conifers in this zone and can grow in pure stands. Mountain hemlock is common in southern Alaska along with Sitka spruce.

Subboreal forest with white spruce hybrids, mountain hemlock, poplar, and birch

Lodgepole pine, Douglas fir, and subalpine fir occur in central British Columbia. Other trees that occur are quaking aspen, balsam poplar, birch, and black cottonwood. The northerly native range of the Devils club shrub (*Oplopanax horridus*) seems to be a good indicator of where the subboreal white spruce zone occurs, before grading into the boreal zone.

Boreal forest. To the north or colder interior areas of the subboreal white spruce hardwood type in Alaska and British Columbia is the boreal white and black spruce zone that extends to the treeless tundra. The forested areas usually have

Boreal forest of Tamarack bog

some combination of white spruce, balsam poplar, quaking aspen, and paper birch. The bog areas usually are dominated by black spruce and tamarack. Subalpine fir and lodgepole pine extend into part of the boreal zone in northwestern Canada. Much of the boreal forest is outside the scope of this book.

Mesic or montane mixed conifer type. This type is in northeastern Washington, southeastern British Columbia, and east to northwestern Montana, which is considered part of the Rocky Mountains (outside the scope of this book). It is below the subalpine type and above ponderosa pine and Douglas fir type. Ten or more tree species can be in one location, creating a rich diversity of species in a small area. Common species include western larch, western white pine, lodgepole pine, Engelmann spruce, subalpine fir, grand fir, Douglas fir, western red cedar, and western hemlock. Hardwoods that can be present include black cottonwood, paper birch, and quaking aspen. Ponderosa pine may appear on drier sites. This type also occurs in the eastern Cascades of Washington and is scattered in the eastern British Columbia coast range. White spruce–Engelmann spruce hybrids can be present in British Columbia. Species diversity decreases going farther north in this type into British Columbia, where it is also referred to as the interior hemlock-cedar zone.

Mesic or montane mixed conifer forest with larch, pine, spruce, fir, and cedar

Redwood forest with redwood trees above a mix of riparian hardwoods

Redwood. The redwood type goes from extreme southwestern Oregon into a large part of northwestern California near and along the coast, and the outer part of the central California coast range. Redwood is the dominant tree, and the tallest stands are slightly offset from the immediate coast. Other trees include Douglas fir, western hemlock, tan oak, California bay, red alder, Santa Cruz cypress, and Shreve oak.

Mixed evergreen forest type. This forest type is found in southwestern Oregon and northwestern California and is scattered throughout the southern coast ranges, western Sierra Nevada, and Southern California mountains. Some of the dominant trees include tan oak, California bay, black oak, canyon live oak, Pacific madrone, Port Orford cedar, incense cedar, ponderosa pine, knobcone pine, redwood, and Douglas fir. Jeffrey pine, sugar pine, and western white pine additionally occur in this type at low elevations in the Klamath-Siskiyou Mountains on serpentine. Other trees with more localized distributions include bristlecone fir (central California coast range), Sargent cypress, California nutmeg, and giant chinquapin.

Mixed conifer forest type. Mixed conifer is found in southwestern Oregon and throughout mountainous areas of California. It frequently borders a mixed evergreen forest and is below the true fir type. Primary species in this type are ponderosa pine, incense cedar, white fir, sugar pine, Jeffrey pine, and black oak. Douglas fir is common in south-central Oregon, northwestern California, and the northern Sierra Nevada. Baker cypress occurs here in parts of northern and northeastern California. Giant sequoia occurs in this type in the central and southern Sierra Nevada.

Oak woodlands type. This area extends from the Puget Sound in Washington, parts of the Columbia River Gorge, and through several valleys in Oregon to Southern California. Commonly, oak woodlands are open with a grassy-herbaceous understory. Main trees are Oregon white oak, valley oak, blue oak, interior live oak, and coast live oak. Engelmann oak is common in Southern California. Other trees include California bay, California buckeye, gray pine, ponderosa pine, and Douglas fir. Oregon white oak stands can occur along or west of the I-5 highway corridor from southern British Columbia south to Redding, the Columbia Gorge east of Portland, and areas in the Northern California coast ranges. Valley oak seems to replace Oregon white oak from Redding down to Bakersfield in the Sacramento and San Joaquin Valleys. Blue oak and gray pine occur in a fringe surrounding the Sacramento–San Joaquin Valleys above valley oak. Coast live oak is dominant on California coast ranges near the Pacific Ocean.

Ponderosa pine–yellow pine. Main trees include ponderosa pine, Jeffrey pine, and Washoe pine. Ponderosa pine forests are most common east of the Cascades in south-central British Columbia, central and eastern Washington and Oregon and Northern California, and east of the Sierra Nevada in California. Washoe pine stands occur in northeastern California, while Jeffrey pine stands occur in the eastern Sierra Nevada, Southern California mountains, and on scattered serpentine sites in California. Ponderosa pine and Jeffrey pine can occur together in California. Common associates include western juniper, single-needle pinyon, Douglas fir, grand fir, lodgepole pine, incense cedar, white fir, Oregon white oak, black oak, canyon live oak, and quaking aspen. This type frequently occurs right above pinyon-juniper, big sagebrush shrub communities, or perennial grasslands when present east of the Cascades and Sierra Nevada.

Lodgepole pine. Lodgepole pine type is dominant in some areas of eastern Oregon and Washington, and also in high-elevation areas of the Sierra Nevada. Trees occurring with lodgepole pine include ponderosa pine, whitebark pine, western white pine, western larch, mountain hemlock, Engelmann spruce, subalpine fir, and quaking aspen. In addition to the preceding trees, red fir, Sierra juniper, limber pine, and foxtail pine are associates in the Sierra Nevada. Lodgepole pine commonly occupies areas with certain soil edaphic characteristics, like wetlands or rocky soils, and can easily dominate a landscape after wildfires. Lodgepole pine can be long-term seral or climax depending on microclimate and soils. In central British Columbia, it occurs above Douglas fir type and below subalpine type, often codominates with white spruce hybrids, and can be referred to as the subboreal pine-spruce or montane zone.

Pinyon-juniper type. This type includes the driest coniferous woodland on the West Coast. Main species are western or Sierra juniper, single-needle pinyon, Utah juniper, and Rocky Mountain juniper. Other trees include Piute cypress, Baker cypress, California juniper, ponderosa pine, and Jeffrey pine. Western juniper can be the only tree in a large part of central and eastern Oregon. Pinyons and junipers occur together east of the Sierra Nevada, southern San Joaquin Valley, and Southern California mountains. Sagebrush species are common shrubs in pinyon-juniper.

Riparian area with white alders

Riparian forest type includes the trees normally occurring along waterways like rivers, streams, creeks, or wetlands. The main trees are red alder, black cottonwood, balsam poplar (northern Alaska and northern British Columbia), Oregon ash, Fremont cottonwood, plains cottonwood, Goodding and many other willows, white alder, and sycamore. Conifers like western red cedar and Port Orford cedar commonly occur in riparian areas. Lodgepole pine is common in areas with seasonally flooded soils. Engelmann spruce frequently occurs at lower elevations below subalpine forest in riparian areas. Sitka spruce is common in wetlands and also along coastal rivers in the northern half of its range.

Chaparral-influenced woodlands. This covers trees and habitats when chaparral shrubs have a strong or dominant presence as part of the plant community. Bishop pine, knobcone pine, Torrey pine, Monterey pine, and many cypresses occur here, and they are also part of a community type called the closed-cone cypress pine woodlands that are often closely associated with chaparral. Some of the species grow right through the chapparal, while several grow in nearly pure stands surrounded by chaparral. Most of the sites are in California, some are on serpentine or poor soils, while some are on non-serpentine. Knobcone pine and Sargent cypress can have large, nearly pure stands within the chaparral zone. MacNab, Santa Cruz, Cuyamaca, and Tecate cypress have individuals or stands that commonly grow in chaparral. There are several other conifers that grow in chaparral also. Gray pine can occur in nearly pure stands on serpentine or non-serpentine sites where chaparral is the dominant understory. Jeffrey pine occur on serpentine soil, frequently in chaparral and at lower elevations. Parry pinyon occurs primarily in stands of chaparral. Big-cone Douglas fir and Coulter pine occur in chaparral individually or in stands. Bishop pine occurs more often in chaparral stands on the Southern California coast. Chamise, manzanita, ceanothus, and shrubby oaks are common shrubs throughout chaparral. Several taller oaks described in this book occur in chaparral also.

ABIOTIC AND BIOTIC CAUSES OF TREE MORTALITY

Factors influencing failure or death of mature trees are described in this text, but not those that mainly influence seedlings or young trees. Often, two or more abiotic and biotic agents combine to cause tree mortality. Nearly all dead trees have symptoms with foliage that is dead, discolored, or dropped. Many abiotic and biotic issues cause discoloring or death of foliage. The table on biotic issues lists signs and symptoms that are more common for that particular group. The table also lists scientific and common names and list of hosts. Not all plant hosts listed for a particular biotic issue are highly susceptible to death or tree failure; the more susceptible hosts are mentioned in the individual tree descriptions. The biotic issues in the table were compiled from previous literature and can often be a sole factor in tree mortality or failure; the table is not all-inclusive. This manual relates to Level 1 or 2 assessments as described in the *Tree Risk Assessment Manual* by ISA, more than Level 3 assessments. Many of the signs in the biotic and abiotic tables can be seen with Level 1 or 2 assessments. However, factors like vascular wilts and root disease may need a Level 3 assessment.

Trees can suffer mortality from abiotic factors, insects, diseases, and mammals. If all the species are affected, it's usually abiotic (e.g., herbicides). If one or two species of trees in a landscape are dying or dead where several tree species occur, the cause is often biotic (e.g., western pine beetle).

There are several ways trees can die due to abiotic causes. Many abiotic causes affect all trees to some extent, while a few are species specific. Drought, aeration deficit, windthrow, fire, cold or heat damage, lightning, salt or ion toxicity, herbicides, air pollution, excessive root damage or girdling roots, flooding, and gas injury are a few ways abiotic causes can cause tree mortality. Many of these have similar symptoms but not specific signs. Some abiotic factors mainly affect younger trees or those plants in areas where they are not compatible with the environment. The table on abiotic issues list factors that are known to cause mortality of mature trees.

Drought. Drought is one of the most serious causes of death to trees, especially in California. Conifers appear to be more susceptible. Millions of conifers have died in the southern Sierra Nevada and Southern California mountains due to drought. If the trees were weakened by drought, bark beetles finished off many of them. Heat domes are weather events where unusual extremely hot temperatures occur in areas for short periods of time, contributing to drought but also capable of starting wildfires. Tree scorching (usually non-fatal) from these short-term events occur more often in areas like western British Columbia, western Washington, and northwestern Oregon, where the trees are not used to these high temperatures.

Fire damage. Suppression of wildfires on the West Coast, especially near urban areas, has increased the occurrence of large-scale damaging fires. The Dixie Fire in California in 2021 was the state's largest-ever wildfire. The western Oregon Cascades saw several unusually large wildfires in 2021. Fire that burned trees near power lines or places where failure can cause human or property damage should be assessed. For hardwoods, cambium injury is the most important factor, followed by leaf and crown injury. A hardwood can regrow leaves from a total burned canopy if cambium is not 100% dead. Many hardwoods can also resprout from a top killed tree.

For conifers, crown injury is the most important factor, followed by cambium damage and bark beetle attacks. A conifer with 100% dead canopy is probably dead, including deciduous larches. Only a few conifer species, like coast redwood, can resprout after top kill by a fire. If the fire has burned around the stem on trees, check the bark thickness. Has the original bark thickness been reduced by the fire? A tree that has had its bark significantly burned (deep charring removing original bark texture) to the cambium is usually dead. Thick-barked species like incense cedar, ponderosa pine, sugar pine, western larch, Douglas fir, redwood, giant sequoia, and coast live oak can survive fires to their stem better. Burned trees indicate a high hazard if less than 50% of the bole is intact and medium probability of failure if 50% to 75% of the bole is intact. One way to check if the tree stem is dead is to chip away at the bark and look at the cambium. If the cambium layer is desiccated, brown, and hard all the way around the stem, the tree is dead. If the entire cambium layer is normal-colored for the live cambium of that species, pliable, and moist, it is still alive. If the fire-burned tree is dead and poses a hazard, it is best to remove it quickly. Promptly removing fire-burned conifers can help reduce massive invasions by bark beetles

Closed campground with numerous hazard trees from Riverside fire in Oregon

Two red turpentine beetles with a predatory clerid beetle

Roundheaded borer

(Scolytinae family). Red turpentine beetle (*Dendroctonus valens*) is one of the first bark beetles to attack fire-damaged pines. Beetles in the Buprestidae (flat-headed or metallic borers), Cerambycidae (roundheaded or long-horned borers), and Siricidae (horntails) families also readily attack fire-damaged or killed trees.

Air pollution. Various conifers and hardwoods are susceptible to air pollution. Ponderosa and Jeffrey pines are two of the most susceptible to it and have been impacted in Southern California.

Windthrow. Most trees are susceptible to some type of windthrow. Occasional hurricane-type windstorms along the Pacific Northwest coast (western Washington and western Oregon) have resulted in many thousands of acres littered with fallen trees. The trees can fall entirely, with the main stems broken, or experience only branches being broken. Western hemlock and Sitka spruce seem to have been most susceptible to these large-scale damaging wind events in the Pacific Northwest. Trees fallen by windstorms are usually all in the same direction, as opposed to trees fallen by root rots that usually lie in crisscross patterns. Santa Ana winds in Southern California come in from the Great Basin and travel west into Los Angeles and surrounding areas. These strong winds from the east create hazardous fire conditions, and some events have windthrown thousands of trees.

Insects. The main groups of insects include bark beetles, shoot and wood borers, defoliators, and plant suckers. The bark beetles are the most lethal to trees. They usually kill the tree, while a few wood borers and the ambrosia beetles may cause live stem breakage. Almost all bark beetles and wood borers have larval galleries under the bark and some type of round entry-exit hole in the bark. Most bark beetles leave a round-shaped hole in the stem, while some borers leave D-shaped or oval-shaped holes in the stem. Sometimes reddish-brown or light-colored boring dust from bark beetles or wood borers can be found on the bark or at the base of trees. Many of the bark beetles leave pitch tubes on the stem.

Mountain pine beetle, western pine beetle, fir engraver, pine engraver, and Jeffrey pine beetle are the most lethal to conifers in California when combined with drought. The spruce beetle has been a large problem in Alaska and British Columbia. The exotic emerald ash borer has killed large numbers of ash trees in the eastern United States and is now causing mortality to ash trees on the West Coast. The exotic Asian long-horned beetle has killed some hardwood trees in the eastern United States and now has been found in California. The golden-spotted oak borer, thought to be introduced from Arizona, is an increasing problem for several oak species in Southern California. The exotic invasive shot-hole borer is becoming

Douglas fir tussock moth caterpillar USDA FOREST SERVICE PHOTO BY MONICA GAYLORD

D-shaped exit hole of gold-spotted oak borer on coast live oak

Larvae, adult, pupae of gold-spotted oak borer

Common transverse style beetle gallery on Pacific silver fir

Mountain pine beetle gallery on ponderosa pine

Spruce beetle gallery on white spruce hybrid

more of a problem for certain hardwoods in California and introduces a fungal disease (fusarium dieback), which aids in killing trees. The western oak bark beetle spreads the fungus foamy bark canker (*Geosmithia pallida*). Many beetles introduce a staining fungi that aids in the process of tree mortality. Western spruce budworm has been a destructive defoliator, particularly in the Pacific Northwest in the Blue Mountains of northeastern Oregon. Gypsy or spongy moth has long been a large problem in the East, and attempts to eradicate the introduced gypsy moth in the West are ongoing.

Diseases. The main groups of tree diseases are root, foliar, mistletoe and broom rusts, stem and branch cankers and rusts, heart and sap rots, and vascular. Root diseases are often the most damaging to trees and, because they are underground, can be difficult to diagnose. Root diseases often kill trees outright. A live tree with root disease is unstable when its roots have extensive decay and can cause failure. A pocket of slowly dying conifers is often a symptom of root disease. Sometimes root diseases result in resin stains on the bark above- and below-ground with resin-soaked wood underneath the bark. Some root diseases grow white hyphal mats under the bark. Port Orford cedar root disease has been very damaging to that species and is reducing the number of individuals or stands in its native range. Dutch elm disease is a vascular wilt disease that has killed millions of elms in the eastern United States but has had minor impact on introduced elms on the West Coast. Stem rusts and cankers nearly always leave some type of visible canker on the main stem or larger branches, and they can cause tree mortality or live stem breakage. Sudden-death oak disease has killed millions of trees in California alone, with tan oak, coast live oak, black oak, and Shreve oak being very susceptible. White pine blister rust has killed millions of five-needle pines in the western United States. Heart rot fungi decay the nonliving wood in the tree stem and can result in stem breakage. Brown rots primarily attack the cellulose, leaving a hard brown cubical appearance, and white rots attack and remove more of the lignin, leaving a white stringy rot. Red ring rot, Indian paint fungus, and sulfur fungus are common and widespread heart rot fungi on conifers and hardwoods. Conifers with multiple red ring rot or Indian paint conks and conifers and hardwoods with sulfur fungus conks indicate a high failure hazard and should be removed from high-use areas.

The individual tree descriptions include additional heart rot decay fungi that seriously weaken trees and pose a failure hazard. Dwarf mistletoe (*Arceuthobium* species) are small parasitic plants. Large numbers of dwarf mistletoe–infected branches on a conifer can weaken the tree and make it more susceptible to branch or stem breakage. There are numerous species of dwarf mistletoe, and each has a primary conifer host. Oak mistletoe is a true mistletoe (*Phoradendron* species) that is green, can grow to more than 4 feet in diameter, and can cause branch breakage.

Armillaria ostoyae resin flow, mycelia, and mushrooms at the base of a conifer
ROBERT L. EDMONDS

Dwarf mistletoe of Jeffrey pine

Indian paint fungus on western hemlock

Red ring rot conks on Douglas fir
USDA FOREST SERVICE PHOTO BY WILLIAM C. WOODRUFF

Sudden oak death staining and leaking sap on a tan oak trunk CHRISTOPHER LEE

White pine blister rust ROBERT L. EDMONDS

Forest decline. This is an issue referring to tree mortality occurring at abnormal rates. The trees appear to die without an obvious cause, however, are usually killed by abiotic or biotic agents or both. Much of the research done has been in Europe and the eastern United States. The declines tend to occur with a single species, but multiple species can be affected also. On the Pacific coast, some of the species that have had unexpected die-offs in the past century from this are Alaska yellow cedar, ponderosa pine, quaking aspen, and western white pine (pole blight).

Hazardous trees. All large dead trees should be considered hazardous. Even though some dead trees, like giant sequoia, can stand dead for decades, all large dead trees are dangerous when near targets. Live trees with heartwood or sapwood conks or large cankers should be considered dangerous to nearby structures or campers. Large old oak trees, especially those with visible hollow branch attachments, are often hazardous. If a conifer has pouch fungus conks (*Cryptoporus volvatus*) on it, the tree is dead under each conk and is potentially hazardous. Animals like the American beaver, or insects like the carpenter worm, can cause enough damage at the base of a tree for potential or imminent failure. Forked trees with large stems above sharp V-shaped attachments and included bark below the attachment are more likely to break at the "V" when exposed to strong winds or heavy loads, as opposed to U-shaped attachments without included bark. Any very large extended horizontal branch should be considered hazardous. A large tree or branch with a deep open crack is hazardous.

Trees with a pronounced lean, especially when the roots and soil opposite the lean are lifting up, can pose an imminent threat of failure. Dead tops of true firs, hemlocks, spruces, and hardwoods are more likely to fail in the near future than those of cedars, redwood, giant sequoia, or junipers. The literature says dead tops or whole pine trees can last long, but I have seen dead tops and whole trees of pine species fail soon after mortality. Live trees with extensive trunk or basal decay can fail easier, depending on the species. Carpenter ants, termites, and large cavities can indicate weak and/or decayed wood in the bole. Some species of root rot disease can cause live tree failure. Trees exposed to floods

Extensive heart rot on live western hemlock

Root plate lifting on right side of Sitka spruce   Detailed photo of Sitka spruce root plate lifting

can fail after soil has washed away from the tree bases and roots or when the soil is waterlogged.

If dead trees are in an area free of targets that have significant consequences of failure, they can be kept standing, possibly as wildlife trees. Trees with large dead branches, large horizontal branches, or cracked or otherwise hazardous branches can be mitigated with pruning. Cracked branches and forked stems can sometimes be mitigated by professionals using cables and braces. It is important to remember that any large tree is subject to failure when exposed to strong wind or heavy loading from snow and ice. Sometimes boles of trees with much internal decay sound hollow when struck with a mallet, aiding in tree hazard assessments.

NON-NATIVE, LANDSCAPE TREES, AND HYBRIDS

The non-native invasive trees described in detail in this manual have a large geographic range on the West Coast or are tall, causing persistent problems with electric utility lines. Black locust, tree of heaven, and Siberian elm are found throughout much of the United States. *Eucalyptus* spp. are more localized in California but can grow tall very fast and frequently need to be pruned back. Mexican fan palm is more common in the southern half of California and causes problems with power lines by growing underneath them, dead fronds drifting onto power lines and trees bending during high winds and contacting lines. English walnut orchards continually need to be trimmed back from power lines. The following are some other non-native invasive trees that are not described in this book. Silver wattle (*Acacia*) is common along the California and Oregon coasts, while pepper (*Schinus*) is common in the southern half of California. Norway maple and horse chestnut (*Aesculus*) are becoming more widespread in the Pacific Northwest. Silver maple is invasive on the Snake and Columbia River drainages in eastern Washington and eastern Oregon. Salt cedar is a highly invasive shrub-tree of riparian areas, especially in desert areas. Russian olive is a short invasive tree, often in riparian areas and colder dry climates. Bird cherry and European mountain ash are short trees invasive in Alaska and south into Washington.

There are too many non-native landscape trees to cover in this manual. It is not uncommon for a landscape tree to have several horticultural varieties, making identification more difficult. I may have missed mentioning a few that are increasingly becoming more invasive. There are numerous non-native pines and oaks used in landscaping on the West Coast. Pines can usually be identified to genus by having one to five needles wrapped in a sheath, while oaks can be readily identified to genus when acorns are present. A few other common tall landscaping trees include ashes, maples, poplars, willows, and palms. Ashes can be identified by opposite, compound leaves and straight-winged samara fruit. Most maples are identified by opposite, lobed leaves and curved-winged samara fruit. Many poplars have wide or heart-shaped leaves, and a few species have resinous buds. Willows normally have narrow linear-lanceolate leaves and winter buds with a single scale.

Hybrid trees occur in hardwoods and conifers and usually occur where the two parent trees overlap in geographic range. They are difficult to identify to species. They are usually

Leaves of Norway maple

Silver wattle leaves and flowers

Pepper leaves and fruits

Cone of white spruce–Sitka spruce hybrid with four-sided needles and erose cone-scale tips

Linear needles attached singly on grand fir with hybrid features; from eastern Oregon-west-central Idaho

among closely related species in the same genus. It can occur among two trees or a tree and a shrub. The Quercus genus (oaks) usually hybridize within the two groups: white oaks and red oaks. The white oak group has leaves with rounded lobes and includes blue oak, valley oak, Oregon white oak, and Engelmann oak. The red oak group has leaves with acute or spiny lobes and includes black oak, coast live oak, interior live oak, and Shreve oak. An intermediate group

Oak hybrid tree with evergreen to semi-evergreen leaves in Lake County, California

includes canyon live oak. There are spruces that hybridize in Alaska and British Columbia. There are true firs that hybridize in Oregon and Northern California. The cottonwood-poplars hybridize and some of the pines also. It appears that apparent hybrids can show up in areas where both parent trees are not located. Examples are in eastern Oregon (Baker-Union Counties) and west-central Idaho where grand fir grows, but the trees have upturned needles and white stomata on the upper surface of the needles, indicating white fir. According to white fir (*Abies concolor-lowiana*) range maps, white fir occurs hundreds of miles from those locations.

WILDLIFE USES

Wildlife uses trees often for food and shelter, and there are numerous examples. Bears and porcupines remove the bark of trees to eat the sapwood. Beavers gnaw down trees with their teeth to alter their habitats and build homes. Conifer cones, acorns, and many fruits are used by animals for food. Animals commonly help disperse seeds, which can enhance regeneration of trees and establish them in new areas. Conifer needles and hardwood leaves are food for animals like elk and moose. Live or dead trees provide shelter for small mammals, birds, bats, lizards, and salamanders. Dwarf mistletoe brooms, which grow in trees, can provide safe nests for birds and squirrels. Most bird nests in trees are protected under the Migratory Bird Treaty Act of 1918. One of the provisions of the act is that it is illegal to harass young birds or take eggs from an active nest without a permit. Canada has the Migratory Birds Convention Act of 1917, which also protects bird nests. There are numerous survey protocols for various eagles, hawks, owls, and smaller songbirds. These protocols are useful for determining the presence or absence of birds and their nests before any man-made activities or disturbances occur in those areas.

REFERENCE TABLES

TREE SPECIES		
Family	**Scientific Name**	**Common Name**
Aceraceae		
	Acer negundo	Box elder
	Acer glabrum	Rocky Mountain maple
	Acer macrophyllum	Big-leaf maple
	Acer platanoides	Norway maple
	Acer saccharinum	Silver maple
Anacardiaceae		
	Pistacia ssp.	Pistache
	Schinus ssp.	Pepper
Arecaceae		
	Washingtonia filifera	California fan palm
	Washingtonia robusta	Mexican fan palm
	Phoenix canariensis	Canary Island palm
Betulaceae		
	Alnus incana	Mountain or thinleaf alder
	Alnus rubra	Red alder
	Alnus rhombifolia	White alder
	Betula kenaica	Kenai birch
	Betula neoalaskana	Resin or paper birch
	Betula occidentalis	Water birch
	Betula papyrifera	Paper birch
Cupressaceae		
	Calocedrus decurrens	Incense cedar
	Chamaecyparis lawsoniana	Port Orford cedar
	Chamaecyparis nootkatensis	Alaska yellow cedar
	Cupressus guadalupensis var. *forbesii*	Tecate cypress
	Cupressus arizonica	Arizona, Cuyamaca, Piute cypress
	Cupressus bakeri	Baker cypress
	Cupressus goveniana	Gowen, Mendocino, Santa Cruz cypress
	Cupressus macnabiana	McNab cypress
	Cupressus macrocarpa	Monterey cypress
	Cupressus sargentii	Sargent cypress
	Juniperus californica	California juniper
	Juniperus grandis	Sierra juniper

Family	Scientific Name	Common Name
Cupressaceae		
	Juniperus occidentalis	Western juniper
	Juniperus osteosperma	Utah juniper
	Juniperus scopulorum	Rocky Mountain juniper
	Sequoia sempervirens	Redwood
	Sequoiadendron giganteum	Giant sequoia
	Thuja plicata	Western red cedar
Elaeagnaceae		
	Elaeagnus angustifolia	Russian olive
Ericaceae		
	Arbutus menziesii	Pacific madrone
Fabaceae		
	Robinia pseudoacacia	Black locust
	Gleditsia triacanthos	Honey locust
	Acacia dealbata	Silver wattle
Fagaceae		
	Chrysolepis chrysophylla	Giant chinquapin
	Lithocarpus densiflorus	Tan oak
	Quercus agrifolia	Coast live oak
	Quercus chrysolepis	Canyon live oak
	Quercus douglasii	Blue oak
	Quercus engelmannii	Engelmann oak
	Quercus garryana	Oregon white oak
	Quercus kelloggii	Black oak
	Quercus lobata	Va
	Quercus parvula var. shrevei (formerly *Quercus wizlizenii*)	Shreve oak
	Quercus tomentella	Island oak
	Quercus wislizeni	Interior live oak
Hippocastanaceae		
	Aesculus californica	California buckeye
	Aesculus hippocastanum	Common horse chestnut
Juglandaceae		
	Juglans regia	English walnut
	Juglans californica	Southern black California walnut
	Juglans hindsii	Northern black California walnut
	Carya illinoinensis	Pecan
Lauraceae		
	Umbellularia californica	California bay

(continued)

Family	Scientific Name	Common Name
Myricaceae		
	Myrica californica	Pacific wax myrtle
Myrtaceae		
	Eucalyptus camaldulensis	Red gum
	Eucalyptus cladocalyx	Sugar gum
	Eucalyptus globulus	Blue gum
	Eucalyptus sideroxylon	Red iron bark
	Eucalyptus leucoxylon	White iron bark
Oleaceae		
	Fraxinus latifolia	Oregon ash
	Fraxinus velutina	Velvet ash
	Fraxinus pennsylvanica	Green ash
Pinaceae		
	Abies amabilis	Pacific silver fir
	Abies bracteata	Bristlecone fir
	Abies lowiana	White fir
	Abies grandis	Grand fir
	Abies lasiocapra	Subalpine fir
	Abies magnifica	Red fir
	Abies procera	Noble fir
	Larix lariciana	Tamarack
	Larix lyallii	Subalpine larch
	Larix occidentalis	Western larch
	Picea breweriana	Brewers spruce
	Picea engelmannii	Engelmann spruce
	Picea glauca	White spruce
	Picea mariana	Black spruce
	Picea sitchensis	Sitka spruce
	Pinus albicaulis	Whitebark pine
	Pinus attenuata	Knobcone pine
	Pinus contorta	Lodgepole pine
	Pinus coulteri	Coulter pine
	Pinus flexilis	Limber pine
	Pinus jeffreyi	Jeffrey pine
	Pinus monophylla	Single-leaf pinyon
	Pinus monticola	Western white pine
	Pinus muricata	Bishop pine
	Pinus ponderosa	Ponderosa pine
	Pinus quadrifolia	Parry or 4-needle pinyon pine

Family	Scientific Name	Common Name
Pinaceae		
	Pinus radiata	Monterey pine
	Pinus sabiniana	Gray pine
	Pinus torreyana	Torrey pine
	Pinus washoensis	Washoe pine
	Pseudotsuga macrocarpa	Big-cone Douglas fir
	Pseudotsuga menziesii	Douglas fir
	Tsuga heterophylla	Western hemlock
	Tsuga mertensiana	Mountain hemlock
Platanaceae		
	Platanus racemosa	California sycamore
Rhamnaceae		
	Frangula purshiana	Cascara
Rosaceae		
	Prunus padus	Bird cherry
	Sorbus aucuparia	European mountain ash
Salicaceae		
	Populus angustifoia	Narrowleaf cottonwood
	Populus balsamifera	Balsam poplar
	Populus deltoides spp. monolifera	Plains cottonwood
	Populus fremontii	Fremont cottonwood
	Populus tremuloides	Quaking aspen
	Populus trichocarpa	Black cottonwood
	Salix amygdaloides	Peachleaf willow
	Salix gooddingii	Black willow
	Salix lasiandra	Pacific willow
	Salix leavigata	Red willow
	Salix scouleriana	Scouler's willow
Simaroubaceae		
	Ailanthus altissima	Tree of heaven
Tamaricaceae		
	Tamarix spp.	Tamarisk
Taxaceae		
	Torreya californica	California nutmeg
	Taxus brevifolia	Pacific yew
Ulmaceae		
	Ulmus pumila	Siberian elm
	Ulmus americana	American elm

BIOTIC CAUSES OF MATURE TREE DEATH OR LIVE TREE FAILURE

Scientific Name	Common Name	Host
	MAMMALS	
Castor canadensis	American beaver	Hardwoods and few conifers
Ursus americanus	Black bear	Many trees
	INSECTS	
	Foliar	
Acleris gloverana	Western black-headed budworm	Several conifers
Choristoneura biennis	Two-year-cycle budworm	Several conifers
Choristoneura occidentalis	Western spruce budworm	Several conifers
Coloradia pandora	Pandora moth	Pines
Lambdina fiscellaria lugubrosa	Western hemlock looper	Several conifers
Lymantria dispar	Gypsy or spongy moth	Hardwoods and conifers
Malacosoma disstria	Forest tent caterpillar	Hardwoods
Melanolophia imitata	Green-striped forest looper	Mainly conifers
Neodiprion tsugae	Hemlock sawfly	Western hemlock
Neophasia menapia	Pine butterfly	Several conifers
Orgyia pseudotsugata	Douglas fir tussock moth	Several conifers
Phyllocnistis populiella	Aspen serpentine leaf miner	Populus
	Leaf, buds, and branch sucking insects	
Adelges piceae	Balsam woolly adelgid	True firs
Glycaspis brimblecombei	Red-gum lerp psyllid	Eucalyptus spp.
Lycorma delicatula	Spotted lanternfly	Tree of heaven and others
	Stem	
Agrilus anxius	Bronze birch borer	Birches
Agrilus burkei	Flatheaded borer	Alders
Agrilus auroguttatus	Golden-spotted oak borer	Oaks
Agrilus planipennis	Emerald ash borer	Ash
Anoplophora glabripennis	Asian long-horned borer	Hardwoods
Dendroctonus brevicomis	Western pine beetle	Ponderosa and Coulter pine
Dendroctonus jeffreyi	Jeffrey pine beetle	Jeffrey pine
Dendroctonus ponderosae	Mountain pine beetle	Pines
Dendroctonus pseudotsugae	Douglas fir beetle	Douglas fir and western larch
Dendroctonus rufipennis	Spruce beetle	Spruce
Dinapate wrightii	Palm borer	Palms
Dryocoetes confusus	Western balsam bark beetle	Few conifers
Euwallacea spp.	Invasive shot-hole borer	Many plants
Ips confusus	Pinyon Ips beetle	Pinyons

Symptoms	Signs & Symptoms
Downed trees near waterways	Girdled hourglass-shaped trunks, downed trees on a water dam
Usually trees attacked while bark is still thin	Bark stripped from stem, large tooth marks going with the grain of the wood
Trees of similarly related species defoliated or otherwise affected by one attack; usually current year foliage or older foliage is attacked, foliage discolored or altered	Minor differences among defoliators
	Chewed discolored foliage, larvae, webbing
	Chewed discolored foliage, larvae, webbing
	Chewed discolored foliage, larvae, webbing
	Chewed discolored or missing foliage, larvae
	Chewed discolored foliage, larvae, webbing
	Chewed discolored foliage, larvae, webbing
	Chewed discolored shriveled foliage, larvae, pupae cases or webbing
	Chewed discolored foliage, larvae, webbing
	Chewed discolored foliage, larvae, cocoons
	Chewed discolored foliage, larvae, pupae cases
	Chewed discolored foliage, larvae, cocoons and webbing
	Larval mines with black frass between leaf surfaces
Differs among these insects	Differs among these insects
Branch swelling, deformation, stunted growth, scattered dead branches	White cottony tufts, purple-brown nymphs
Immature leaf drop, sticky leaves on ground	Honeydew, black sooty mold, waxy caplike lerps on leaves
Immature leaf drop, honeydew buildup on ground	Honeydew, black sooty mold, oozing with fermented odor
Dead trees of similarly related species, trees weakened by abiotic factors like drought or fire, holes in stems with or without pitch, discolored or dropped foliage	Exit holes that are round, D-shaped, or oval
	D-shaped holes in stem, rust-colored sap
	D-shaped holes in stem, sap
	D-shaped holes in stem, bark staining and bleeding
	D-shaped holes in stem
	Boring dust and pitch streamers
	Boring dust and pitch tubes
	Boring dust and pitch tubes
	Boring dust and pitch tubes
	Boring dust and pitch streamers
	Boring dust and pitch streamers
	Trunk buckling where wood has been eaten away
	Boring dust and pitch streamers
	Boring dust, staining, gumming, white powdery exudate
	Boring dust and pitch tubes

(continued)

Scientific Name	Common Name	Host
INSECTS (continued)		
Ips paraconfusus	California five-spined Ips	Pines
Ips pini	Pine engraver	Pines
Megacyllene robiniae	Locust borer	Black locust
Melanophila drummondi	Flatheaded fir borer	Firs, few conifers
Monarthrum spp.	Oak ambrosia beetle	Fagaceae
Phloeosinus spp.	Cedar or juniper bark beetle	Cupressaceae
Prionoxystus robiniae	Carpenter worm	Hardwoods
Pseudohylesinus granulatus	Fir root bark beetle	Few conifers
Pseudohylesinus nobilis	Noble fir bark beetle	Noble fir
Pseudohylesinus sericeus	Silver fir bark beetle	Few conifers
Pseudopityophthorus pubipennis	Western oak bark beetle	Hardwoods
Saperda calcarata	Poplar borer	Salicaceae
Scolytus ventralis	Fir engraver beetle	True firs
Xyleborus monographus	Mediterranean oak borer	Several oaks
DISEASES		
Foliar		
Elytroderma deformans	Elytroderma needle cast	Ponderosa and lodgepole pine
Phaeocryptopus gaeumannii	Swiss needle cast	Douglas fir
Rhizoctonia butunii	Web blight	Several conifers
Buds and branches		
Arceuthobium spp.	Dwarf mistletoe	Many conifers
Melampsorella caryophyllacearum	Fir broom rust	True firs
Chrysomyxa arctostaphyli	Spruce broom rust	Spruces
Phytophthora palmivora	Phytophthora bud rot	Palms
Thielaviopsis paradoxa	Thielaviopsis trunk or bud rot	Palms
Stem vascular diseases		
Fusarium oxysporum	Fusarium wilt	Variety of plants
Ophiostoma ulmi	Dutch elm disease	Elms
Verticillium albo-atrum and *V. dahliae*	Verticillium wilt	Hardwoods
Stem rusts and cankers		
Atropellis piniphila	Atropellis canker	Ponderosa and lodgepole pine
Ceratocystis fimbriata	Black canker	Populus
Coryneum cardinale	Cypress canker	Cupressaceae
Cronartium comandrae	Comandra blister rust	Ponderosa and lodgepole pine
Cronartium ribicola	White pine blister rust	5-needle pines
Cryptosphaeria ligniota	Cryptosphaeria canker	Aspen
Cytospora spp.	Cytospora canker	Conifers and hardwoods
Encoelia pruinosa	Sooty bark canker	Hardwoods

Symptoms	Signs & Symptoms
	Boring dust and pitch tubes
	Boring dust and pitch tubes
	Boring dust
	Oval-shaped holes in stem
	Whitish to reddish-brown boring dust
	Boring dust and pitch tubes
	Boring dust and fecal pellets
	Boring dust
	Boring dust
	Boring dust
	Boring dust, clear or creamy-colored sap
	Boring frass, oozing sap
	Boring dust and pitch streamers
	Boring dust and oozing sap
Differs among foliar diseases	Differs among foliar diseases
Branch flagging, clumps of reddened needles	Brooms and black fruiting bodies
Sparse crown, needle loss	Mottled needles and black fruiting bodies
Browning of outer foliage in circular areas	Fungal webbing on infected leaves
Differs among diseases	Differs among diseases
Growth loss, distortion and swelling, top kill	Plants with scalelike leaves and rounded fruits, brooms
Chlorotic shortened needles, dead or broken tops	Yellowish brooms, cankers
Chlorotic shortened needles, dead or broken tops	Yellowish brooms, cankers
Young leaf discoloration and wilting, bud and meristem rot	Leaf bases are necrotic with foul odor
Young leaf discoloration and wilting, bud and meristem and trunk rot	Leaf bases are necrotic with foul odor
Wilting and leaf scorch are common for xylem attacked species; chlorosis, stunting and witches broom are common for phloem attacked species	Differs among vascular wilts
	Reddish-brown internal tissue
	Brown streaking in sapwood
	Sapwood streaking or banding
Wounds on trees indicate potential disease entry, dead branches, localized area of sunken tissue	Differs among rusts and cankers
	Long and narrow cankers with blue stained sapwood
	Blackened elliptical-shaped canker with varnished appearance
	Cankers with resin-discolored branches
	Cankers with swellings, resin, and rust-colored spores
	Diamond-shaped cankers with sap and yellow-to-orange pustules
	Long, narrow cankers with orange-brown margin, dark inner bark
	Sunken cankers with oozing orange spores
	Canker revealing blackened sapwood, becoming powdery

(continued)

BIOTIC CAUSES OF MATURE TREE DEATH OR LIVE TREE FAILURE (continued)

Scientific Name	Common Name	Host
DISEASES (continued)		
Endocronartium harknessii	Western gall rust	2- and 3-needle pines
Fusarium circinatum	Pitch canker	Several pines
Geosmithia morbida	Thousand cankers disease	Walnuts
Hypoxylon mammatum and spp.	Hypoxylon cankers	Hardwoods
Inonotus spp.	Canker rots	Primarily oaks, also several other hardwoods
Nattrassia mangiferae	Arbutus canker	Madrone and other plants
Neofusicoccum arbuti	Madrone canker	Madrone and other plants
Phytophora cactorum	Crown canker	Madrone and other hardwoods
Phytophthora ramorum	Sudden oak death	Hardwoods and other plants
Stem decay		
Echinodontium tinctorium	Indian paint fungus	True firs and hemlocks
Fomes fomentarius	White spongy trunk rot	Several hardwoods
Fomitopsis officinalis	Brown trunk rot	Several conifers
Fomitopsis pinicola	Brown crumbly rot	Hardwood and conifers
Ganoderma applanatum and other spp.	Ganoderma trunk and root rot	Hardwoods, conifers, palms
Inonotus spp.	Canker rots	Primarily oaks, also several other hardwoods
Laetiporus sulphureus and spp.	Sulfur fungus	Conifers and hardwoods
Perenniporia fraxinophila	White mottled rot	Ashes
Phaeolus schweinitzii	Schweinitzii butt and root rot	Conifers and hardwoods
Phellinus ignarius	Phellinus trunk rot	Several hardwoods
Phellinus robustus	White trunk rot	Hardwoods and conifers
Phellinus tremulae	False tinder fungus	Aspen
Porodaedalea pini (Phellinus pini) and spp.	Red ring rot	Conifers
Roots		
Armillaria spp.	Armillaria root disease	Hardwoods and conifers
Heterobasidion occidentale (Fomes annosus)	Heterobasidion root disease (Fir annosus)	Firs, spruces, hemlocks, sequoia
Heterobasidion irregulare (Fomes annosus)	Heterobasidion root disease (Pine annosus)	Pines, incense cedar, juniper
Leptographium wageneri	Black stain root disease	Conifers
Onnia tomentosa	Tomentosus root rot	Conifers
Phaeolus sulphurascens	Laminated root rot	Several conifers
Phytophora cinnamomi and spp.	Phytophthora crown and root rot	Variety of plants
Phytophora lateralis	Port Orford cedar root disease	Port Orford cedar and yew

Symptoms	Signs & Symptoms
	Cankers and galls with orange pustules
	Cankers with oozing sap
	Black or brown cankers
	Cankers with gray-black fungal tissue
	Conks, fruiting bodies, swollen or sunken torn areas on stem
	Sunken cankers
	Blackened stem and branches
	Cankers, black sap, sapwood discoloration
	Cankers seeping black or red ooze
Large wounds on trees indicate potential disease entry, internal rot visible on broken stems, white or brown decay	Conks of various colors and shapes
	Dark hoof-shaped conks with hard teeth or spines on lower surface
	Grayish to dark hoof-shaped conks with a whitish undersurface
	Grayish hoof-shaped conks, elongated with age
	Dark bracket-shaped conks with reddish margin and whitish undersurface
	Reddish-brown bracket-shaped conks with a whitish undersurface
	Conks, fruiting bodies, swollen or sunken torn areas on stem
	Large clustered shelflike soft conks, yellow-to-orange colored
	Dark bracket-shaped conks with whitish undersurface
	Dark mushroom-like conks that are velvety on upper surface
	Grayish-to-black hoof-shaped conks with a brownish and velvety undersurface
	Dark bracket-shaped conks with whitish undersurface
	Grayish-to-black hoof-shaped conks with purple-brown undersurface
	Dark hoof-shaped conks with irregular pored undersurface
Groups of dead trees or groups of downed trees fallen in different directions, trees dying from the bottom up, decreased growth, crown deterioration, chlorosis	Differs among root diseases
	Fungal hyphae on sapwood and roots, basal resin flow, golden brown-colored mushrooms
	Discolored wood, conks, occasional basal resin flow
	Discolored wood, conks, occasional basal resin flow
	Basal resin flow, dark stained sapwood
	Yellow-brown fruiting bodies, red-brown staining of wood
	Live windthrown trees, fungal hyphae on roots
	Discolored sapwood, dark stained bleeding stem and cankers
	Cinnamon-colored sapwood

ABIOTIC CAUSES OF MATURE TREE DEATH OR LIVE TREE FAILURE

Factor	Location	Signs	Outcome
Air Pollution	More common in Southern California Los Angeles basin	Individual or groups of dead trees near large urban areas, chlorosis, foliage drops prematurely, reduced growth	Several tree species, several pines are susceptible to tree mortality.
Drought	Common in Pacific coast forests, usually inland, off of the coast	Wilting chlorosis, reddening of foliage, trees die from the top down, commonly with bark beetle signs	Can cause mortality on large tracts of land, more recently in southern Sierra Nevada and Southern California
Fire	Common in Pacific coast forests, except right along the coast	Trees with blackened trunks and dead burned foliage, signs of bark beetles	Can cause mortality on large tracts of land, leaving millions of potentially hazardous trees
Flood	Throughout Pacific coast	Downed or dead trees in flooded areas	Water can wash away soil around roots, leading to live tree failure. Ponded water can cause mortality.
Herbicides	All along Pacific coast	All trees in sprayed area affected, can vary between foliage stunting, chlorosis, necrosis, deformation	Uptake of herbicides through the roots can easily cause tree mortality.
Ion Toxicity	For example, road-salt spray can be common along major highways.	Dead or dying trees with discolored foliage only along roadsides	Can cause mortality of trees along roads
Lightning	Throughout Pacific coast	Long vertical scars on the tree trunk	Thorough lightning strike can cause tree mortality.
Wind	Throughout Pacific coast	Groups of downed trees all in the same direction	Historic large-scale wind storms along Pacific Northwest coast

WINTER IDENTIFICATION KEY FOR DECIDUOUS SPECIES

1	Branches with short stubby projections, yellow needles littering ground	Larix, larch	
1	Branches without short stubby projections, leaves littering ground	Hardwoods	2
2	Buds and branches opposite on stems	Acer, Fraxinus, Aesculus	
2	Buds and branches alternate on stems	Alternate-leaves species	

BUDS AND BRANCHES OPPOSITE

1	Large terminal bud with smaller lateral buds, large heart-shaped leaf scar, round fruit	Aesculus, horse chestnut, and buckeye	
1	Similar terminal and lateral buds, leaf scar usually narrower, winged samara fruit in trees		2
2	Leaf scar usually narrow the full length, two curved winged samara attached until maturity	Acer, maple	
2	Leaf scar usually wider in the middle, one straight winged paddle-shaped samara	Fraxinus, ash	

BUDS AND BRANCHES ALTERNATE

1	Multiple buds crowded at branch tips, acorn caps attached to tree branches	Quercus, oaks	
1	Normally single bud at branch tips	Others	2
2	Spines, buds sunken or not sunken in the branch	Robinia, locust - Elaeagnus , Russian olive	3
2	No spines, buds usually not sunken in branch		4
3	Paired spines, buds sunken in the branches, bark not fibrous and peeling, legume-type fruit	Robinia, locust	
3	Occasional spines, buds not sunken but bumpy, fibrous peeling bark, berries and young twigs with whitish scales	Elaeagnus, Russian olive	
4	Mottled whitish stem where bark fell off, thin U-shaped leaf scar circling bud, spherical fruits with numerous projections	Platanus, sycamore	
4	Fruit, bud scar, and bark different	Others	5
5	Hard nut fruits on ground or in tree, hairy buds, interior of twig cut lengthwise has pith chambered	Juglans, walnut	
5	Different fruit, lacking interior pith chambered	Others	6
6	Thick branches with large heart-shaped or shield-shaped leaf scar, twisted samara fruits on tree	Ailanthus, tree of heaven	
6	Twig and scar smaller	Others	7
7	Elongated bud with short stalk, both catkins and cones may be present on tree	Alnus, alder	
7	Bud different	Others	8
8	Peeling bark that is usually whitish, sometimes copper colored, both catkins and cones may be present on tree	Betula, birch	
8	Bark is non-peeling	Others	9
9	Globular buds having scale margins with long white hairs, fruit is circular winged samara	Ulmus pumila, Siberian elm	
9	Buds and bud scale margins differ	Others	10
10	Sticky yellow-orange or reddish-orange stained resinous scented buds, except quaking aspen	Populus, cottonwoods	
10	Non-resinous buds	others	11
11	Whitish bark with black scarring and black cankers	Populus, quaking aspen	
11	Other bark without black scarring	Others	12
12	Narrow leaves and buds have single scale	Salix, willow	
12	Narrow to ovate leaves, buds have multiple scales, lenticelled bark that is ill scented beneath (Prunus), dried berries on trees	Prunus, cherry - Sorbus, mountain ash	
12	Oblong to ovate leaves, buds have no scales but are hairy and fuzzy, fruit is a drupe	Frangula, cascara	

(continued)

BUDS AND BRANCHES ALTERNATE (ALTERNATE OR OPTIONAL KEY)

1	Bark whitish, mottled or not, smooth when young and sometimes when mature		2
1	Bark not whitish, usually grayish, and somewhat furrowed or fibrous with age		8
2	Mottled whitish stem where bark fell off, thin U-shaped leaf scar circling bud, spherical fruits with numerous projections	Platanus, sycamore	
2	Bark mottled or not, fruits not spherical with numerous projections		3
3	Elongated bud with short stalk, both catkins and conelike fruit may be present on tree	Alnus, alder	
3	Buds on twigs not stalked		4
4	Peeling bark that is usually whitish, sometimes copper colored, both catkins and cone-like fruit may be present on tree	Betula, birch	
4	Bark is not peeling and whitish		5
5	Sticky yellow-orange or reddish-orange stained resinous scented buds, bark turns gray and furrowed with age	Populus, cottonwoods	
5	Buds are not color-stained and resinous		6
6	Whitish bark with black scarring and black cankers	Populus, quaking aspen	
6	Mottled bark without black cankers and scarring		7
7	Buds have multiple scales	Sorbus, mountain ash	
7	Buds do not have scales but are hairy and fuzzy	Frangula, cascara	
8	Multiple buds crowded at branch tips, acorn caps attached to tree branches	Quercus, oaks	
8	Usually single bud at branch tip		9
9	Spines, buds sunken or not sunken in the branch	Robinia, locust—Elaeagnus, Russian olive	10
9	Normally no spines on branch		11
10	Occasional spines, buds not sunken but bumpy, fibrous peeling bark, berries with whitish scales	Elaeagnus, Russian olive	
10	Paired spines on branches, buds sunken in branches, legume fruit pods	Robinia, locust	
11	Hard-nut fruits on ground or in tree, hairy buds, interior of twig cut lengthwise has pith chambered	Juglans, walnut	
11	Different type of fruit, twig pith not chambered		12
12	Thick branches with large heart-shaped or shield-shaped leaf scar, twisted samara fruits on tree	Ailanthus, tree of heaven	
12	Branches usually thinner and without large heart-shaped leaf scar		13
13	Globular buds having scale margins with long white hairs, fruit is circular winged samara	Ulmus pumila, Siberian elm	
13	Buds do not have both globular and long white hairs on margins, different fruit		14
14	Narrow leaves and buds have single scale	Salix, willow	
14	Narrow to ovate leaves, buds have multiple scales, lenticelled bark, ill scented beneath bark (Prunus), dried berries on trees	Prunus, cherry—Sorbus, mountain ash	
14	Oblong to ovate leaves, buds without scales, bark can be plain gray, lenticelled, or mottled	Frangula, Cascara	

PHYLUM KEY

1	Trees with seeds borne in an ovary	Angiosperms (monocot or dicot)
	Leaves are very large palmate or pinnately divided with parallel veins	Monocots (family Arecaceae, palms)
	Leaves are simple or compound with pinnate veins and with an obvious midrib and often with side veins	Dicots (hardwood trees)
2	Trees with seeds not borne in an ovary	Gymnosperms (conifers)

FAMILY KEYS

Three groups of gymnosperms

1	Gymnosperm leaves are short and scalelike or needle-like, some cones with peltate scales	Cupressaceae
2	Gymnosperm with needles and berry or leathery cone without scales	Taxaceae
3	Gymnosperm with needles and woody cones without peltate scales	Pinaceae

Key for Dicot families

Four groups of dicots separated by leaf type and arrangement (families within five groups separated on fruit type)

A	Dicots with alternate simple evergreen leaves	
	Fruit is an acorn nut with a scaly cap or a spiny covering	Fagaceae
	Fruit is capsule, leaves not scalelike but larger and lanceolate to rounded	Myrtaceae (Eucalyptus)
	Fruit is capsule, leaves are short and scalelike and are unique in this regard for angiosperms in this book	Tamaricaceae (Tamarix)
	Fruit is a legume	Fabaceae (some species of Acacia)
	Fruit is a berry, leaves entire, lanceolate, and strongly scented	Lauraceae (Umbellularia)
	Fruit is a berry, leaves oblong, entire to serrulate, and not scented	Ericaceae (Arbutus)
	Fruit that is usually a drupe or pome not covered in bumps, leaves usually ovate and not scented	Rosaceae (Prunus)
	Fruit is a drupe covered with bumps, leaves narrowly oblanceolate and wavy margined and scented	Myricaceae (Myrica)
B	Dicots with alternate simple deciduous leaves	
	Fruit is circular winged samara, leaves with serrated margins	Ulmaceae
	Fruit is capsule formed on catkins, leaves with smooth, serrate, or crenate margins	Salicaceae
	Fruit is conelike or a catkin with winged seeds, leaves with serrated margins, bark usually whitish	Betulaceae
	Fruit is an acorn	Fagaceae (Quercus)
	Fruit is spheric achene covered with projections	Platanaceae
	Fruit is a drupe, leaves and fruit have whitish scales and stellate hairs, tree occasionally thorny	Elaeagnaceae (Elaeagnus)
	Fruit is usually a drupe or pome, leaves usually serrate, lacking silvery scales, bark usually lenticelled, not mottled	Rosaceae (Prunus)
	Fruit is a drupe, leaves entire or serrulate, oblong to ovate, lacking silvery scales, bark usually mottled, occasionally softly lenticelled	Rhamnaceae (Frangula)
C	Dicots with opposite or palmate leaves that are deciduous	
	Fruit is straight-winged single samara, mostly compound leaves with smooth or serrate margined leaflets	Oleaceae (Fraxinus)
	Fruit is curve-winged double samara, simple, or compound leaves with lobed or dentated margins on leaves or leaflets	Aceraceae (Acer)
	Spheric capsule fruit is with or without prickles, palmate leaves with serrated margined leaflets	Hippocastanaceae (Aesculus)
D	Dicots with alternate compound leaves that are deciduous or evergreen	
	Fruit is twisted-winged samara, deciduous leaves with smooth margined leaflets	Simaroubaceae (Ailanthus)

(continued)

	Fruit is legume, deciduous or evergreen leaves with smooth margined leaflets	Fabaceae
	Fruit is hard nut, deciduous leaves with smooth or serrated margins on the leaflets	Juglandaceae
	Fruit is a drupe, mostly evergreen leaves with smooth to serrated margins on the leaflets	Anacardiaceae
	Fruit is a pome, mostly deciduous leaves with serrated margins on the leaflets	Rosaceae (Sorbus)

Optional or Alternative Key for Dicot families

Continuation for Dicot families, separated more by leaf type

A	Dicots with alternate simple evergreen leaves	
1	Leaves are short and scalelike and are unique in this regard for angiosperms in this book, fruit is capsule	Tamaricaceae (Tamarix)
1	Leaves are linear to ovate, fruit is variable	2
2	Leaves are usually linear, fruit is a legume	Fabaceae (some species of Acacia)
2	Leaves lanceolate to ovate, fruit is variable	3
3	Leaves are scented, fruit is a capsule, trees are non-native	Myrtaceae (Eucalyptus)
3	Leaves and fruit are variable, trees are native	4
4	Leaves are variable, fruit is a nut (acorn)	Fagaceae
4	Leaves are variable, fruit is drupe, pome, or berry	5
5	Fruit is a berry	6
5	Fruit is a drupe	7
6	Leaves entire, lanceolate, and strongly scented, fruit is a berry	Lauraceae (Umbellularia)
6	Leaves oblong, entire to serrulate and not scented, fruit is a berry	Ericaceae (Arbutus)
7	Leaves usually ovate and not scented, fruit is usually a drupe or pome	Rosaceae (Prunus)
7	Leaves narrowly oblanceolate and wavy margined and scented, fruit is a drupe covered with bumps	Myricaceae (Myrica)
B	Dicots with alternate simple deciduous leaves	
1	Leaves entire or lobed, fruit is a nut (acorn) with a scaly cap	Fagaceae (Quercus)
1	Leaves serrate, entire or lobed, fruit variable	2
2	Leaves are lobed, fruit is a spheric achene covered with projections	Platanaceae
2	Leaves are serrate or entire and not deeply lobed, fruit variable	3
3	Leaves are serrate, fruit is a circular-winged samara	Ulmaceae
3	Leaves are serrate or entire, fruit variable	4
4	Leaves entire, fruit is a drupe, plant has whitish scales and stellate hairs, non-native	Elaeagnaceae (Elaeagnus)
4	Leaves are entire or serrate, fruit variable, no whitish scales, mostly native trees	5
5	Leaves with some serration, fruit is a drupe or pome	6
5	Leaves serrate or entire, fruit is a capsule, cone, or catkin-like	7
6	Leaves with margins various, bark usually with lenticels, fruit is usually a drupe or pome	Rosaceae (Prunus)
6	Leaves entire or serrulate, bark usually mottled, fruit is a drupe	Rhamnaceae (Frangula)
7	Leaves entire, serrate, or crenate, fruit is capsule formed on catkins, bark grayish or whitish	Salicaceae
7	Leaves with serrated margins, fruit is conelike or catkin-like with winged seeds, bark usually whitish	Betulaceae
C	Dicots with opposite or palmate leaves that are deciduous	
1	Palmate leaves with serrated margined leaflets, spheric capsule fruit is with or without prickles	Hippocastanaceae (Aesculus)
1	Opposite; simple or compound leaves with smooth, dentated, or lobed margins, fruit is straight- or curved-winged samara	2
2	Opposite; simple or compound leaves with smooth- or serrate-margined leaflets, fruit is straight-winged single samara	Oleaceae (Fraxinus)

2	Opposite; simple, or compound leaves with lobed or dentated margins, fruit is curve winged double samara	Aceraceae (Acer)
D	Dicots with alternate compound leaves that are deciduous or evergreen	
1	Mostly evergreen leaves with linear to oblong leaflets, fruit is a drupe	Anacardiaceae
1	Deciduous leaves with smooth or serrated margined leaflets (evergreen leaves for Acacia)	2
2	Deciduous or evergreen leaves with smooth-margined leaflets, fruit is a samara or legume	3
2	Deciduous leaves with smooth- or serrate-margined leaflets, fruit is a pome or hard nut	4
3	Deciduous leaves with smooth-margined leaflets, fruit is twisted-winged samara	Simaroubaceae (Ailanthus)
3	Deciduous or evergreen leaves with smooth-margined leaflets, fruit is legume	Fabaceae
4	Deciduous leaves with smooth or serrated margins on the leaflets, fruit is hard nut	Juglandaceae
4	Mostly deciduous leaves with serrated margins on the leaflets, fruit is a pome	Rosaceae (Sorbus)

GENUS KEYS

Anacardiaceae

	Leaves persistent, leaflets linear and serrated or toothed	Schinus, pepper
	Leaves deciduous, leaflets lanceolate and entire	Pistachia, pistache

Arecaceae (Palms)

	Leaf fronds pinnate	Phoenix
	Leaf fronds fanlike	Washingtonia

Betulaceae

1	Trees with peeling whitish bark, fruit disintegrates at maturity	2
1	Trees with whitish bark not peeling, fruit persistent at maturity	3
2	Bark copper colored turning pinkish or white, leaves 3–8 cm glabrous to sparsely short hairy, mainly boreal zone of Alaska and Canada	Betula neoalaskana, resin birch
2	Bark copper colored turning pinkish to whitish, leaves 4–5 cm sparsely to moderately short hairy, mainly Alaska	Betula kenaica, Kenai birch
2	Bark copper colored turning whitish, leaves 4–10 cm sparsely to moderately short hairy, occurs in northern Washington and Canada	Betula papyrifera, paper birch
3	Trees with smooth white bark, even with age, growing along coast, double serrated leaves, revolute leaf margins	Alnus rubra, red alder
3	Trees with smooth white bark turning checkered with age, typically single serrated non-revolute leaf margins, normally offset away from coast	Alnus rhombifolia, white alder

Cupressaceae

1	Leaves are in the shape of needles or awl-like, mature trees over 80 meters tall	Sequoia, redwood—Sequoiadendron, giant sequoia
1	Leaves are scalelike	2
2	Round berry-like cone, branches are rounded, usually growing in semidesert environments	Juniperus, junipers
2	Round cones with peltate scales, branches are rounded, most species have an affinity to growing on poor soils, except Monterey cypress	Cupressus, cypresses
2	Cones with or without peltate scales, branches are somewhat flattened, usually growing in mixed forests and growing to tall trees	Calocedrus, Chamaecyparis, Thuja, (cedars)

Fabaceae

	Leaves single pinnate, leaflets 2–4 cm, tree usually with spines, flowers in racemes	Robinia, black locust
	Leaves bipinnate, leaflets 1.5–2.5 cm, tree usually without spines in landscaping, flowers in racemes	Gleditsia, honey locust
	Leaves bipinnate or simple linear, leaflets on pinnate leaves less than 1 cm, trees with or without spines, flowers in spherical clusters	Acacia

(continued)

Fagaceae

Nuts enclosed in spiny capsule appendage, leaves entire and yellowish beneath	Chrysolepis chrysophylla, giant chinquapin
Acorn caps with projecting scales, leaves serrated or occasionally entire, hairy to whitish beneath	Lithocarpus, tan oak
Acorn caps with appressed scales, leaves lobed, toothed or entire, various beneath	Quercus, oaks

Juglandaceae

Trees have an oblong fruit, leaves with 9–17 curved lanceolate leaflets	Carya illinoinensis, pecan
Trees have a round fruit, leaves with 11–19 straight to slightly curved lanceolate leaflets	Juglans hindsii and californica, California black walnut
Trees have a round fruit, leaves with 5–11 straight elliptic to oval leaflets	Juglans regia, English walnut

Pinaceae

1	Needles deciduous, clustered on stout pegs on branches	Larix
1	Needles evergreen, attached singly or in fascicles	2
2	Needles in fascicles of 1–5	Pinus
2	Needles not in fascicles, attached singly	3
3	Cones are upright and break apart on tree at maturity; buds rounded (except Abies bracteata)	Abies
3	Cones are pendant and fall to the ground without breaking apart	4
4	Needles single and dull pointed, cones pendant with pitchfork bracts beneath cone scales; buds pointed	Pseudotsuga
4	Needles single, cones pendant without pitchfork bracts beneath scales	5
5	Needles single, cones pendant, needles blunt, flexible, and usually less than 1 inch long, non-scaly bark that is furrowed and ridged	Tsuga
5	Needles single, cones pendant, needles stiff, and most are sharp pointed, scaly Bark	Picea

Rosaceae

Alternate simple leaves, fruit is a drupe	Prunus
Alternate compound leaves, fruit is a pome	Sorbus

Salicaceae

Trees with single-scaled winter bud, leaves lanceolate and usually more than 2X longer than wide	Salix
Trees with multiscaled winter bud, leaves usually ovate and usually less than 2X longer than wide (except narrowleaf cottonwood)	Populus

Taxaceae

Trees with stiff, spine-tipped needles, cone is berry-like with hard leathery skin and 3–4 cm, scattered in California	Torreya, California nutmeg
Trees with pointed, more flexible needles, not spine tipped, cone is berry-like with soft skin and 1 cm, commonly occurs in older forests on Pacific coast	Taxus, Pacific yew

SPECIES KEYS

Abies (most species with foliage that are scented different among others Abies)

1	Needles sharp pointed	Bristlecone fir
1	Needles round tipped	2
2	White stomata on lower surface only	3
2	White stomata on upper and lower surfaces	4
3	Needles flattened and spreading forward in 180-degree arc	Pacific silver fir
3	Needles flattened on both sides of branches	Grand fir
4	Needles normally flattened on lower part of tree and curved on upper part of tree	white fir

4	Needles curved throughout tree	5
5	Lower needles on individual branches bent near base	6
5	Lower needles on individual branches not bent near base	subalpine fir
6	Cones with exserted bracts, thin bark in short rectangular gray to purplish plates	noble fir
6	Cones with no exserted or partially exserted bracts, bark reddish brown in long vertical furrows, thick	red and Shasta fir

Acer

1	Leaves are opposite and compound, lobed or unlobed	Box elder
1	Leaves are opposite and simple, lobed	2
2	Leaves 6 inches or shorter, acuminate leaf projections scattered on leaf edges, bark smooth to having shallow vertical ridges	Norway maple
2	Leaves 6 inches or larger, leaf lobes usually with blunt tips, bark is furrowed with long vertical ridges	Big-leaf maple
2	Leaves 6 inches or shorter, leaf is deeply incised and leaf lobes have acute pointed teeth, bark kind of scaly, paired samaras usually unequal	Silver maple

Aesculus

	Invasive tree, spiny fruit, more commonly in Pacific Northwest	Common horse chestnut
	Native shrub or small tree, non-spiny fruit, mainly in California	California buckeye

CEDARS: Calocedrus, Chamaecyparis, Thuja (all four cedars have distinctively different scents on foliage)

1	Plants have cones with non-peltate scales	2
1	Plants have round cones with peltate scales	3
2	Plants have cones 2–3 cm long, internode leaf scales are long, no X patterns of white stomata on underside of branch	Calocedrus, incense cedar
2	Plants have cones 1–2 cm long, internode leaf scales are short, there are usually X patterns of faint white stomata on underside of branch	Thuja, western red cedar
3	Plants have heavily drooping branches and often grow in subalpine habitat, weak or no X patterns of white stomata on underside of branch	Chamaecyparis, Alaska yellow cedar
3	Plants have slightly drooping branches and often grow in non-subalpine habitats, strong X patterns of white stomata on underside of branch	Chamaecyparis, Port Orford cedar

Cupressus (Species Derived from the Flora of North America)

1	Tree with asymmetric or flattened crown, growing naturally or introduced along coastline	Monterey cypress
1	Tree normally with symmetric crown, resin-covered glands on leaf scales	2
1	Tree normally with symmetric crown, without or rarely with resin-covered glands on leaf scales	3
2	Cone scales with straight conic projections, northeastern and Northern California near Oregon	Baker cypress
2	Cone scales with straight or curved conic projections, usually in serpentine surrounding Sacramento Valley in Northern California	MacNab cypress
2	Cone scales with straight conic projections, Kern County and Cuyamaca Mountains in San Diego County, California	Arizona cypress
3	Bark various, central California coast, three subspecies	Gowen, Santa Cruz, Mendocino,
3	Bark is fibrous, usually serpentine sites in California coast ranges	Sargent cypress
3	Bark is peeling revealing red brown smooth trunk, Otay Mountain in San Diego County and Santa Ana Mountains in Orange County, California	Tecate cypress

Eucalyptus

	Tree with persistent furrowed bark, red flowers	Eucalyptus sideroxylon, red iron bark
	Tree with peeling bark, flowers white, yellow, or pink	2
2	Inflorescence with 1 flower/fruit per leaf axil, occurs up and down California Coast	blue gum, Eucalyptus globulus

(continued)

2	Inflorescence with two or more flowers/fruits per leaf axil	3
3	Leaves can be less or more than 15 cm, bark persistent near base, peeling above, San Joaquin Valley and Southern California	Red gum, Eucalyptus camaldulensis
3	Leaves usually less than 15 cm, bark peeling in smalls strips or plates, white flowers, Southern California	Sugar gum, Eucalyptus cladocalyx
3	Leaves usually less than 15 cm, bark peeling in large strips, white or pink flowers, Southern California	White ironbark, Eucalyptus leucoxylon

Fraxinus		
	Leaves have 5–7 leaflets ovate to obovate, usually sessile	Oregon ash
	Leaves have 5–7 leaflets lanceolate to ovate, usually stalked and hairy when young, native to Southern California	Velvet ash
	Leaves have (5) 7–9 leaflets lanceolate, stalked, non-native landscaping trees	Green ash

Juniperus (all Junipers here have toothed scale margins at 20 X magnification except Rocky Mountain juniper)		
1	Shrub- or treelike	2
1	Usually treelike and single stemmed	3
2	Shrublike, gland obvious on scales, California	California juniper
2	Tree- or shrublike, gland not obvious on scales, California and Nevada	Utah juniper
2	Tree- or shrublike, with scale glands usually without resin, bark brownish, northeastern Oregon, Washington, British Columbia	Rocky Mountain juniper
3	Tree with obvious scale glands and resin, bark brownish, northeastern California and eastern Oregon	Western juniper—var. occidentalis
3	Tree with obvious scale glands and resin, bark reddish brown, mainly Sierra Nevada and Southern California mountains	Sierra juniper—var. australis

Larix		
	Tall tree of Douglas fir–grand fir communities, twigs slightly tomentose to glabrous	Western larch
	Shorter tree of subalpine communities, twigs strongly tomentose	Alpine larch
	Tree of boreal forests, especially bogs, twigs glabrous	Tamarack

Picea		
1	Needles are two-sided or somewhat flattened in cross section	2
1	Needles are three- or four-sided or square in cross section	3
2	Needles are sharp pointed with needle-like tip, grows primarily along the coast	Sitka spruce
2	Needles are blunt pointed, growing in mountains of southwestern Oregon and northwestern California	Brewer spruce
3	Twigs are glabrous, tree mainly growing in boreal forests in Alaska, Canada, and Rocky Mountain locations in the United States	White spruce
3	Twigs are somewhat hairy, habitat variable	4
4	Twigs are short bristly hairy, trees occur in subalpine habitats in the United States and Canada	Engelmann spruce
4	Twigs are hairy, trees occur in boreal forests, usually below subalpine forests and in bogs	Black spruce

Pinus		
1	Small, nearly globular cones, usually in semidesert areas with junipers	Pinyons 2
1	Diversity of cones and habitats, but usually in mountains or along coast	Pines 3
2	Needles in fascicle of one	Single-leaf pinyon
2	Needles in fascicles of two	Two-needle pinyon

2	Needles in fascicles of four, occasionally two, three, or five	Parry or four-needle pinyon
3	Trees occurring along the Pacific coastline	4
3	Trees normally occurring inland, away from the Pacific coastline	5
4	Needles in fascicles of two, needles 2–8 cm, cones 2–6 cm	Shore pine (Pinus contorta var. contorta)
4	Needles in fascicles of two, needles 10–15 cm, cones 5–10 cm, whorled and persistently closed on stems	Bishop pine
4	Needles in fascicles of three, needles 10–15 cm, cones 6–18 cm, whorled and persistently closed on stems	Monterey pine
4	Needles in fascicles of 5 on mature tree, needles 15–25 cm, cones 15 cm, only along coast of San Diego County	Torrey pine
5	Needles in fascicles of two	Lodgepole pine (var. murrayana and latifolia)
5	Needles in fascicles of three or five	6
6	Needles in fascicles of three	7
6	Needles in fascicles of five	11
7	Cones 6–18 cm with a thick knob tip and whorled and persistently closed on stems	Knobcone pine
7	Cones with thick recurved scale tips or slender prickles	8
8	Cones with thick recurved scale tips	9
8	Cones with slender prickles	10
9	Heavy cones, 20–35 cm, yellow brown with thick recurved scale tips, Southern California	Coulter pine
9	Heavy cones, 10–30 cm, brownish with thick recurved scale tips, northern 2/3 of California	Gray pine
10	Cones 7–10 cm, symmetric with variable prickles on scale tips	Washoe pine
10	Cones 7–15 cm, often asymmetric with outcurved prickles on scale tips	Ponderosa pine
10	Cones 13–25 cm, symmetric with straight to incurved prickles on scale tips	Jeffrey pine
11	Cones 3–9 cm, breaking apart at maturity on tree, somewhat curved and stiff Needles	Whitebark pine
11	Cones not breaking apart at maturity	12
12	Cone scale tips without a prickle	13
12	Cone scale tips with a prickle	14
13	Cones 20–60 cm, twisted flexible needles	Sugar pine
13	Cones 9–25 cm, straight flexible needles	Western white pine
13	Cones 7–15 cm, somewhat curved and stiff needles	Limber pine
14	Cones 5–15 cm with scale tip prickle less than 1 mm, subalpine habitats	Foxtail pine
14	Cones 5–15 cm with scale tip prickle 1–6 mm, only White Mountains in California-Nevada in this book	Bristlecone pine

Pinus (ALTERNATE OR OPTIONAL KEY)

1	Small, nearly globular cones, usually in semidesert areas with junipers	Pinyons 1
1	Diversity of cones and habitats, but usually in mountains or along coast	Pines 3
2	Needles in fascicle of one	Single-leaf pinyon
2	Needles in fascicles of two	Two-needle pinyon
2	Needles in fascicles of four, occasionally two, three, or five	Parry or four-needle pinyon
3	Pines with needles in groups of twos	4
3	Pines with needles in groups of threes	5
3	Pines with needles in groups of fives	6

(continued)

PHYSICAL IDENTIFICATION KEY FOR ALL SPECIES (continued)

4	Cones 2–6 cm, needles 2–8 cm	Lodgepole or shore pine
4	Cones 5–10 cm, needles 5–15 cm	Bishop pine
5	Heavy cones, 20–35 cm, yellow brown with thick recurved scale tips, Southern California	Coulter pine
5	Heavy cones 10–30 cm brownish with thick recurved scale tips, northern 2/3 of California	Gray pine
5	Cones 7–15 cm, often asymmetric with outcurved prickles on scale tips	Ponderosa pine
5	Cones 13–25 cm, symmetric with straight to incurved prickles on scale tips	Jeffrey pine
5	Cones 6–18 cm, whorled and persistently closed on stems, scale tip knob greater than 2 cm	Knobcone pine
5	Cones 6–18 cm, whorled and persistently closed on stems, scale tip knob less than 2 cm	Monterey pine
6	Cones 20–60 cm, twisted flexible needles	Sugar pine
6	Cones 9–25 cm, straight flexible needles	Western white pine
6	Cones 7–15 cm, somewhat curved and stiff needles	Limber pine
6	Cones 3–9 cm, breaking apart at maturity on tree, somewhat curved and stiff needles	Whitebark pine
6	Cones 5–15 cm, with prickle on cone scale tip, short clustered needles, subalpine habitats	Bristlecone and foxtail pine
6	Needles in fascicles of five on mature tree, cones 15 cm, with prickle on cone scale tip, only along coast of San Diego County	Torrey pine
	Populus	
1	Non-resinous, non-scented winter bud, persistent white bark, ovate leaves with short pointed tips	Quaking aspen
1	Resinous scented winter buds, leaves cordate to ovate to lanceolate	2
2	Leaves lanceolate to narrowly ovate, occurs in southeastern California but more common in southern Rocky Mountains	Narrowleaf cottonwood
2	Leaves cordate to ovate	3
3	Leaves cordate with short pointed tip, found primarily at lower elevations at Pacific coast locations	4
3	Leaves ovate to cordate with longer evenly tapered tip, habitat variable	5
4	Occurs in California and east into Arizona, fruit capsule round or spherical	Fremont cottonwood
4	Occurs in eastern Oregon and eastern Washington, east to Rocky Mountains and eastern United States, fruit capsule ovoid or pear shaped	Plains cottonwood
5	Ovate leaves with long pointed tip, occurs from California north to British Columbia and southern Alaska, fruit capsule with three or four valves	Black cottonwood
5	Ovate leaves with long pointed tip, occurs in interior Alaska and northern British Columbia, fruit capsule with two valves	Balsam poplar
	Pseudotsuga	
	Needles are scented, cones 10 cm, grows throughout Pacific coast except Southern California	Douglas fir
	Needles usually non-scented, cones 15 cm, grows in Southern California	Big-cone Douglas fir
	Quercus (lists native [non-hybrid] trees over 10 m [35 feet] tall)	
1	Leaves deeply lobed	2
1	Leaves shallowly or not lobed	4
2	Lobes are rounded	3
2	Lobes are pointed	Black oak
3	Acorn nut is 30–50 mm long with pointed tip, oak woodland in Sacramento–San Joaquin Valleys and California coast ranges	Valley oak
3	Acorn nut is 20–30 mm long with rounded tip, western Oregon and Washington, mixed evergreen forest in California	Oregon white oak
4	Leaves glabrous and shiny beneath	5

4	Leaves not glabrous and shiny beneath	6
5	Leaves concave and green beneath, with spiny tips, coast live oak, coast ranges and Southern California	Coast live oak
5	Leaves not concave and yellow green beneath (2–5 cm), margins spiny or smooth, throughout California	Interior oak
5	Leaves not concave and olive green beneath (3–9 cm), margins spiny or smooth, mainly near the California coast	Shreve oak
6	Leaves dull colored beneath, not noticeably hairy	7
6	Leaves hairy or whitish beneath	8
7	Leaves shallow-lobed, mainly oak woodlands surrounding Sacramento–San Joaquin Valleys	Blue oak
7	Leaves not lobed, mainly Southern California oak woodlands	Engelmann oak
8	Leaves golden hairy or whitish beneath, spiny or smooth margins, mixed evergreen forests throughout California	Canyon live oak
8	Leaves densely hairy beneath, spiny margins, Southern California	Coast live oak var. oxyadenia

Salix

1	Leaves not glaucous underneath, overlapping bud scale margins, Southern California east to Arizona	Goodding willow
1	Leaves glaucous underneath	2
2	Trees with glaucous leaves on underside, overlapping bud scale margins, mainly California	Red willow
2	Trees with mostly glaucous leaves on underside, overlapping bud scale margins, central Washington and Oregon east to Rockies	Peachleaf willow
2	Trees with mostly glaucous leaves on underside, non-overlapping bud scale margins, Pacific coast north to Canada and east to Rockies	Pacific willow

Sequoia and Sequoiadendron Redwood and giant sequoia

	Trees with needle-like leaves in flattened planes on branches, north and central California coast	Redwood
	Trees with awllike leaves growing around stems, in Sierra Nevada	Giant sequoia

Tsuga

	Needles are in flattened planes on branches in different lengths, cone 2–3 cm long	Western hemlock
	Needles are spiraled on branches in more or less equal lengths, cone 5–7 cm	Mountain hemlock

Ulmus

	Leaves 3–8 cm equal at base, winter bud is spherical with white hairy scale margins	Siberian elm
	Leaves 8–15 cm unequal at base, winter bud is often pointed, without white hairy scale margins	American elm

Washingtonia

	Invasive tree with slender trunk tapering to swollen base	Mexican fan palm
	Native tree with thicker trunk not normally swollen, southeastern California desert	California fan palm

PACIFIC SILVER FIR
Abies amabilis

Look For: For quick identification, look for a conical symmetric crown with flattened dark-green spreading needles, upright purplish cones, and smooth to scaly or plated bark.

Bark: The trunk is smooth and light gray with resin blisters when young. Mature trees have gray bark with scales and shallow furrows.

Needles: The needles are flattened, equally spreading forward, dark green above, and 2–4.5 cm (0.75–1.75 inches) long. The needles on the lower surface are a lighter green with 2 bands of white stomata.

Cones: The cone is upright, purplish, and 9–17 cm (3.5–6.5 inches) long. The cones break apart at maturity before falling to the ground.

Height: It commonly grows 30–45 m (100–150 feet) tall, occasionally up to 70 m (235 feet) tall. It has trunk diameters of 0.9–1.2 m (3–4 feet), occasionally up to 2.3 m (7.5 feet) wide.

Range: Pacific silver fir is a true fir that occurs from southeastern Alaska through western British Columbia, Washington, and Oregon to northwestern California. This includes the coast ranges, Cascades, and northwestern California mountains.

Habitat: It grows in Douglas fir–hemlock–cedar, true fir, subalpine forests from 0 to 1,500 m (0–4,900 feet) in the northern part of its range and 1,000–2,300 m (3,300–7,500 feet) in the southern part of its range. It does not usually occur in drier forests in the eastern Cascades with ponderosa pine.

Associated Species: It is commonly associated with trees like subalpine fir, noble fir, Pacific silver fir, western hemlock, western red cedar, Douglas fir, mountain hemlock, lodgepole pine, western white pine in most of its range, and incense cedar, Shasta red fir, and Brewer spruce (northwestern California) in the southern part of its range.

Similar Trees: Other similar firs include Douglas fir and true firs like grand and white. Douglas fir has pendant cones with pitchfork bracts extending from beneath the scales in the cone. Douglas fir needles also grow out radially from all around the twigs. Grand fir has flattened needles on all except the uppermost cone branches. White fir has green to whitish-green needles that are flattened below on the tree and curved upward higher in the tree. Western hemlock has shorter needles and pendant

Pacific silver fir with other firs and mountain hemlock

Bark

Cones

Needles

cones. Noble fir has blue-green glaucous needles that are turned upward. The crushed needles of Pacific silver fir have a distinct mild scent that differs from that of Douglas fir and the other true firs.

Tree Risk Hazard Assessment

Biotic and Abiotic Factors: There are several factors that can cause mortality of Pacific silver fir, including insects and diseases such as Heterobasidion root disease, Cytospora canker, Pacific silver fir beetle, fir engraver beetle, fir root bark beetle, and balsam woolly adelgid. Other signs that indicate a live tree may have high failure potential include one or more conks on the main stem (especially Indian paint fungus). Pacific silver fir is very sensitive to fires.

GRAND FIR
Abies grandis

Look For: For quick identification, look for conical symmetrical crown with dark-green flattened needles with white stomata on the lower surfaces, upright green to light-brown cones, and grayish bark with cracks and shallow fissures.

Bark: The trunk is grayish with vertical cracks and shallowly furrowed with age.

Needles: The needles are green, white stomata on lower surfaces only, and flattened on all but the highest cone bearing branches, 3–6 cm (1–2.5 inches) long.

Cones: The cone is upright, green to light brown at maturity, 6–12 cm (2.5–5 inches) long. The cones break apart at maturity before falling to the ground.

Height: It commonly grows 40–60 m (130–200 feet) tall, occasionally up to 70 m (230 feet) tall. It has trunk diameters of 0.5–1 m (1.5–3.5 feet), occasionally up to 2 m (6.5 feet) wide. It tends to grow taller on the coast than inland.

Range: Grand fir is a true fir that occurs from southern British Columbia south through Washington and Oregon to the Northern California coastline. From the Pacific Ocean it occurs east through northern Idaho to northwestern Montana. This includes the Cascades, coast ranges, and northern Rocky Mountains.

Habitat: It grows in Douglas fir–hemlock–cedar, coastal, Douglas fir–grand fir, ponderosa forests at low to middle elevations from 0 to 1,800 m (0–6,000 feet). It is uncommon to absent in subalpine forests.

Associated Species: It is commonly associated with trees like Sitka spruce, Douglas fir, western hemlock, western red cedar, incense cedar, redwood, western larch, lodgepole pine, western white pine, ponderosa pine, Port Orford cedar (southwestern Oregon), and hardwoods like red alder, black cottonwood, bigleaf maple, Oregon white oak, and madrone.

Similar Trees: Other similar firs include Douglas fir and true firs like white and silver. Douglas fir has pendant cones with pitchfork bracts extending from beneath the scales in the cone. Douglas fir needles also grow out radially from all around the twigs. Pacific silver fir needles are flattened and spreading forward. White fir has flattened needles on lower stems, but most of the tree has upturned needles. White fir also has bands of stomata on both needle surfaces. Western hemlock has shorter needles and pendant cones. Grand fir can hybridize with white fir where they cross ranges in the Oregon Cascades and Northern

Grand fir in ponderosa pine forest

Bark

Cones

Needles

California, making identification difficult. Eastern Oregon also appears to have grand fir with characteristics of white fir, like upcurved needles on branches and white stomata on upper surface of needles. The crushed needles of grand fir have a distinct scent that differs from that of Douglas fir and the other true firs.

Tree Risk Hazard Assessment

Biotic and Abiotic Factors: There are several factors that can cause mortality of grand fir, including insects and diseases such as Heterobasidion root disease, armillaria root disease, laminated root rot, Douglas fir tussock moth, western spruce budworm, western balsam bark beetle, and fir engraver beetle. Other signs that indicate a live tree may have high failure potential include one or more conks on the main stem (especially Indian paint fungus).

SUBALPINE FIR
Abies lasiocarpa

Look For: For quick identification, look for symmetrical, spire-shaped crown with needles turned upward with stomata on both surfaces, short upright purplish to blue-gray cones, and smooth to cracked-shallow furrowed bark.

Bark: The trunk is smooth and light gray with resin blisters when young. Mature trees have gray bark with shallow furrows.

Needles: The needles are turned upward, light green to blue green with bands of stomata on both surfaces and 2.5–3 cm (1–1.2 inches) long. There are minor differences in the needle scars and twig bud scales that separate this from the Rocky Mountains *Abies bifolia*.

Cones: The cone is upright, purplish to grayish blue and 5–12 cm (2–5 inches) long. The cones break apart at maturity before falling to the ground.

Height: It commonly grows 18–30 m (60–100 feet) tall, occasionally up to 50 m (160 feet) tall. It has trunk diameters of 45–60 cm (18–24 inches), occasionally up to 2 m (6.5 feet) wide.

Range: Subalpine fir is a true fir that occurs from southeastern Alaska and Yukon, south through British Columbia, Washington, and Oregon to northwestern California. From the Pacific Ocean, it occurs east to western Alberta south through the Rockies to New Mexico. Depending on author, *Abies lasiocarpa* includes the Pacific coast ranges, Cascades, and northwestern California mountains. *Abies bifolia* occurs throughout most of the Rocky Mountains from Yukon to Arizona and New Mexico. This book covers *Abies lasiocarpa* on the Pacific coast.

Habitat: It grows in subboreal white spruce hardwood, lodgepole pine, true fir, and subalpine forests from 0 to 1,050 m (0–3,500 feet) in the northern part of its range, and 1,200–2,100 m (4,000–7,000 feet) in the southern part of its range.

Associated Species: It is commonly associated with trees like Engelmann spruce, whitebark pine, Pacific silver fir, western hemlock, western red cedar, grand fir, Douglas fir, mountain hemlock, lodgepole pine, western white pine, quaking aspen in most of its range, subalpine larch in the northern Cascades, white spruce, balsam poplar, paper birch in British Columbia, and, additionally, Shasta red fir and Brewer spruce in the southern part of its range.

Similar Trees: Other similar firs include Douglas fir and true firs like noble, white,

Abies lasiocarpa
Abies bifolia

Bark

Cones

Two subalpine firs in riparian meadow

and Shasta red. Douglas fir has pendant cones with pitchfork bracts extending from beneath the scales in the cone. Douglas fir needles also grow out radially from all around the twigs. Noble, shasta, and red fir have glaucous blue-green needles that are curved and bent upward, but the lower needles on the stem are bent in the shape of a hockey stick. Noble and Shasta red fir have exserted bracts

Needles

beneath the cone scales. White fir has whitish-green needles that are flattened, longer below on the tree, and curved upward higher in the tree. Mountain hemlock has shorter needles and pendant cones. The crushed needles of subalpine fir have a distinct scent that differs from that of the other true firs and conifers.

Tree Risk Hazard Assessment

Biotic and Abiotic Factors: There are several factors that can cause mortality of subalpine fir, including insects and diseases such as laminated root disease, western balsam bark beetle, western spruce budworm, and balsam woolly adelgid. Other signs that indicate a live tree may have high failure potential include one or more heart rot conks on the main stem (especially Indian paint fungus). Subalpine fir is very sensitive to fires.

CALIFORNIA WHITE FIR
Abies lowiana (concolor)

Look For: For quick identification, look for conical symmetrical crown with green to whitish-green needles (flattened on lower part of tree, curved up on upper part of tree), stomata lines on both surfaces (usually more on lower surfaces), upright light-green to light-brown cones, and grayish bark with irregular vertical-diagonal fissures.

Bark: The trunk is grayish and irregularly furrowed in vertical and diagonal directions.

Needles: The needles are green to whitish green (whitish lines of stomata on both surfaces), flattened on lower branches, crowded and bent upward on higher branches, 3–7 cm (1–3 inches) long. The lower branches may appear to have white stomata only on the lower surfaces of the needles.

Cones: The cone is upright, light green, to light brown at maturity, 7–13 cm (2.5–5 inches) long. The cones break apart at maturity before falling to the ground.

Height: It commonly grows 25–60 m (80–195 feet) tall, occasionally up to 75 m (245 feet) tall. It has trunk diameters of 1–1.5 m (3–5 feet), occasionally up to 4 m (13 feet) wide.

Range: White fir is a true fir that occurs from the mountains in central Oregon south through California to Baja California in Mexico. It also occurs in the Great Basin and Rocky Mountains from Nevada and southeastern Idaho to northern Mexico. *Abies lowiana* occurs from central Oregon to Southern California, depending on author. *Abies concolor* occurs in Nevada, Utah, Idaho, Colorado, New Mexico, and into Sonora, Mexico. Some authors consider the white fir in Oregon and Southern California *Abies concolor*, while that in the Sierra Nevada, *Abies lowiana*. **This book covers the species that occur in Oregon and all of California.**

Habitat: It grows in mixed conifer, true fir, and lower subalpine forests at middle elevations from 600 to 3,000 m (2,000–10,000 feet). It is normally not present in coastal forests.

Associated Species: It is commonly associated with trees like Douglas fir, sugar pine, incense cedar, ponderosa pine, Jeffrey pine, red fir, Port Orford cedar, giant sequoia (southern Sierra Nevada), and hardwoods like black oak, canyon live oak, and tan oak.

Similar Trees: Other similar firs include Douglas fir and true firs like grand, subalpine, noble, red, and silver. The two species of Douglas fir have pendant cones with pitchfork bracts extending from beneath the scales in the cone. Douglas fir needles also grow out radially from all around the twigs and have pointed buds, as opposed to rounded buds. Noble, red, Shasta red, and subalpine firs do not have flattened needles on the lower stems. Silver fir needles are flattened but are green on top and spreading forward, and equally spreading on lower stems. Grand fir has flattened needles on all except the uppermost cones branches and are dark green above and have two

California white fir with Jeffrey pines

lines of white stomata beneath. Grand fir hybridizes with white fir where they cross ranges in the Oregon Cascades and Northern California, making identification difficult. The crushed needles of white fir have a mild distinct scent that differs from that of Douglas fir and the other true firs.

Tree Risk Hazard Assessment

Biotic and Abiotic Factors: There are several factors that can cause mortality of white fir, including insects and diseases such as Heterobasidion root disease, armillaria root disease, laminated root rot, dwarf mistletoe, Cytospora canker, western spruce budworm, fir engraver

Bark

beetle, and flatheaded fir borer. Other factors of tree failure include one or more conks on the main stem (i.e., Indian paint fungus)

Cones

Needles

Needles

RED FIR AND SHASTA RED FIR
Abies magnifica

Look For: For quick identification, look for conical symmetrical crown with glaucous blue-green needles (combination of somewhat flattened and strongly bent upward growing together), lines of stomata on both surfaces of needles, upright reddish-brown cones, and reddish-brown bark with vertical furrowed rectangular ridges.

Bark: The trunk is smooth and grayish with resin blisters when young. Mature trees have bark dark brown to dark red, furrowed, rectangular vertical ridges.

Needles: The needles are glaucous blue green (stomata on both surfaces), with both somewhat flattened needles and many strongly bent upward, 2–3.5 cm (0.8–1.4 inches) long.

Cones: The cone is upright, green to purplish, and reddish brown at maturity, 9–21 cm (3.5–8.2 inches) long and without exserted cone bracts. Shasta fir has seed cone bracts slightly exserted (tan to greenish) from beneath the cone scales. The cones break apart at maturity before falling to the ground.

Height: It commonly grows 40–60 m (130–200 feet) tall, occasionally up to 75 m (250 feet) tall. It has trunk diameters from 1 to 2 m (3.3–6.5 feet) wide, occasionally up to 3 m (10 feet) wide.

Range: Red fir is a true fir that occurs from the mountains in central Oregon, south to the southern Sierra Nevada range in California. This includes the southern Oregon and northern California Cascades, northwestern California mountains, Northern California coast range, and Sierra Nevada. Shasta red fir occurs mostly in Oregon, Northern California, and the southern Sierra Nevada, while red fir occurs mainly in the southern part of the Cascades and Sierra Nevada of California. Shasta red fir is a hybrid or intermediate between red fir and noble fir.

Habitat: It grows in true fir and subalpine forests from 1,400 to 2,700 m (4,500–9,000 feet).

Associated Species: It is commonly associated with trees like white fir, incense cedar, western white pine, mountain hemlock, Brewer spruce, lodgepole pine, giant sequoia (southern Sierra Nevada), and Pacific silver fir (Oregon Cascades).

Similar Trees: Other similar firs include Douglas fir and true firs like subalpine, noble, white. The two species of Douglas fir have pendant cones with pitchfork bracts extending from beneath the scales in the cone. Douglas fir needles also grow out radially from all around the twigs. Noble fir

has bracts extending out from scales (farther than in Shasta red fir) in the cones and bark with grayish-purplish plates on mature trees. Subalpine fir has generally smoother bark, purplish cones at maturity, and all the needles are bent upward. White fir has flattened needles on the lower branches, a different texture of grayish bark, and different-color cones. The crushed needles of red fir have a distinct scent that is somewhat similar to noble fir but differs from the other true firs and conifers.

Red fir in subalpine forest

Tree Risk Hazard Assessment

Biotic and Abiotic Factors: There are several factors that can cause mortality of red fir, including insects and diseases such as Heterobasidion root disease, armillaria root disease, dwarf mistletoe, Cytospora canker, fir engraver beetle, and flatheaded fir borer. Other signs that indicate a live tree may have high failure potential include one or more conks on the main stem, especially Indian paint fungus.

Cones

Shasta red fir cones

Fir engraver beetles

Bark

Needles

NOBLE FIR
Abies procera

Look For: For quick identification, look for conical symmetrical crown with glaucous blue-green needles (combination of somewhat flattened and strongly bent upward), lines of stomata on both surfaces of needles, upright cones with fully exserted yellowish bracts, and grayish (young trees) to grayish-purplish bark (mature trees) with irregular rectangular shallow furrowed ridges.

Bark: The trunk is smooth and grayish with resin blisters when young. Mature trees have shallow furrowed, irregular rectangular vertical ridges. Bark on old-growth trees can be grayish to purplish.

Needles: The needles are glaucous blue green, with both somewhat flattened needles and many strongly bent upward growing together, 1–3.5 cm (0.5–1.4 inches) long. The lower needles are bent at their bases.

Cones: The cone is upright, purplish at maturity, 10–18 cm (4–7 inches) long. The fully exserted yellow-green seed cone bracts hide most of the cone. The cones break apart at maturity before falling to the ground.

Height: It commonly grows 40–50 m (130–170 feet) tall, occasionally up to 70 m (230 feet) tall. It has trunk diameters of 1–1.5 m (40–60 inches), occasionally up to 2.2 m (7.2 feet) wide.

Range: Noble fir is a true fir that occurs from the mountains in west-central Washington through western Oregon to northwestern California. This includes the Cascades, coast ranges, and Klamath mountains in northwestern California. Noble fir hybridizes with red fir, producing Shasta red fir, a variety somewhat intermediate between the two. Shasta red fir bark appears distinctly different from that of noble fir. Upon personal observation, Shasta red fir appears to be more common than noble fir in the southern Oregon Cascades, which may contradict the range map presented here.

Habitat: It grows in true fir, Douglas fir–hemlock–cedar, and occasionally mixed conifer forests from 700 to 2,400 m (2,300–7,800 feet). It is infrequent in subalpine forests.

Associated Species: Its most common associate is Pacific silver fir, and it is also associated with trees like Douglas fir, western red cedar, western hemlock, mountain hemlock, western larch, Alaska yellow cedar, and Brewer spruce.

Similar Trees: Other similar firs include Douglas fir and true firs like subalpine and Shasta red fir. Douglas fir has pendant cones with pitchfork bracts extending from beneath the scales in the cone. Douglas fir needles also grow out radially from all around the twigs. Red fir and Shasta red fir have bark more reddish brown and deeper furrowed. Red fir has no exserted cone bracts, while Shasta red fir has slightly exserted cone bracts. Subalpine fir has generally smoother bark, purplish cones (no cone bracts) at maturity, and all the needles are bent upward. Pacific silver fir has needles in flattened sprays and are dark green above. The crushed needles of noble fir have a distinct scent that is somewhat similar to red fir but differs from the other true firs and conifers.

Two noble firs in true fir forest

Tree Risk Hazard Assessment

Biotic and Abiotic Factors: There are a few factors that can cause mortality of noble fir, including insects and diseases such as armillaria root disease, fir engraver beetle, and noble fir bark beetle. Other signs that indicate a live tree may have high failure potential include one or more conks on the main stem, especially Indian paint fungus.

Bark

Cones

Needles

BIG-LEAF MAPLE
Acer macrophyllum

Look For: For quick identification, look for a tree with a spreading crown that has gray bark with vertical fissures, large multilobed opposite leaves with usually blunt lobes, deciduous yellow leaves in the fall months, and a winged samara fruit.
Bark: The trunk is grayish with vertical fissures and can also have long narrow rectangular plates.
Leaves: The leaves are green, opposite, deciduous, 15–30 cm (6–12 inches) long, with 5–7 incised lobes.
Fruit: The fruit is a 2 paired winged samara, each 4–5 cm (1.5–2 inches) long.
Height: It commonly grows 15–20 m (50–65 feet) tall and occasionally up to 30 m (100 feet) tall. It has trunk diameters of 0.6–2 m (2–5 feet) and up to 2.5 m (8 feet).
Range: Big-leaf maple occurs from southwestern British Columbia south through western Washington, western Oregon, and coastal California to Southern California. It also occurs in the Sierra Nevada.
Habitat: It grows in riparian, mixed evergreen, oak woodlands, Douglas fir–hemlock–cedar, redwood, and coastal forests from 0 to 2,000 m (0–7,000 feet).
Associated Species: It is commonly associated with hardwoods like black cottonwood, red alder, white alder, canyon live oak, coast live oak, Oregon white oak, California bay, Pacific madrone, tan oak, box elder, sycamore, Fremont cottonwood, willows and conifers like redwood, grand fir, Douglas fir, western hemlock, ponderosa pine, western red cedar, Port Orford cedar, and incense cedar.
Similar Trees: Trees with similar leaves include California sycamore and other maples. Sycamore has a mottled colored trunk and different type of fruit, which is round. Rocky mountain maple is a smaller tree with smaller leaves and acutely pointed leaf lobes. Invasive Norway maple has acuminate leaf projections scattered on the leaf edges. Silver maple has leaf lobes that are acutely pointed and uneven sizes of the paired samara fruit.

Tree Risk Hazard Assessment
Biotic and Abiotic Factors: There are a few factors that can cause mortality of big-leaf maple, including insects and diseases such as armillaria root rot and invasive shot-hole borer. Other signs that indicate a live tree may have high failure potential include one or more conks on the main stem from various heartwood rots.

Big-leaf maple in mixed evergreen forest

Bark

Samara fruit

Leaf

BOX ELDER
Acer negundo

Look For: For quick identification, look for a tree with a spreading crown, possible multistemmed, with opposite compound leaves with or without lobes, irregular furrowed bark bases on larger trees, growing near streams, and a curved winged samara fruit.

Bark: The trunk is grayish and vertically furrowed, becoming more diagonally furrowed at the base of the tree.

Leaves: The leaves are opposite, compound, up to 20 cm (8 inches) long and wide, green, and glabrous. There are usually 3–5 leaflets that are entire, serrated, or lobed and 5–10 cm (2–4 inches) long.

Fruit: The fruit is a 2 paired curved winged samara, each 4–5 cm (1.5–2 inches) long.

Height: It commonly grows 12–15 m (40–50 feet) and sometimes up to 20 m (70 feet) tall. It has trunk diameters of 30–60 cm (1–2 feet) and up to 1 m (3 feet).

Range: Box elder occurs in much of the United States, south-central Canada, Mexico, and Guatemala. In California it occurs mainly in lower-elevation riparian areas, and is apparently introduced in Oregon and Washington.

Habitat: It grows along streams in riparian zones from 0 to 600 m (0–2,000 feet) in California, occasionally higher in elevation.

Associated Species: It is commonly associated with trees like sycamore, valley oak, walnut, white alder, Fremont cottonwood, ashes, and willows.

Similar Trees: Other trees with similar leaf shape are the ashes. The riparian ashes usually have more leaflets, and they are not lobed, and the fruit is a straight winged samara. Walnuts and tree of heaven have more leaflets, which are not partially lobed. Other maple (Acer) trees usually have simple lobed leaves.

Tree Risk Hazard Assessment

Biotic and Abiotic Factors: There are a few factors that can cause mortality of box elder, including insects like invasive shot-hole borer and diseases such as Verticillium wilt. Other signs that indicate that a live tree may have failure potential include one or more conks on the main stem from heart rot.

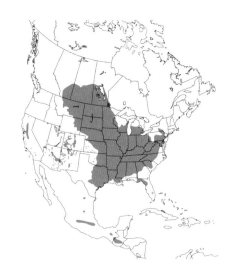

Box elder in riparian area

Bark

Samara fruit

Leaf

TREE OF HEAVEN
Ailanthus altissima

Look For: For quick identification, look for a tree with an open crown, stems usually clustered, compound leaves, somewhat smooth grayish bark, and large clusters of reddish-brown twisted samara fruits.

Bark: The trunk is grayish and slightly roughened with lenticles and vertical tearlike marks.

Leaves: The leaves are alternate, pinnately compound, green, and 50–60 cm (20–25 inches) long. Each leaf has 13–25 lanceolate leaflets that are toothed at the base and 7–13 cm (2.5–5 inches) long.

Fruit: The fruit is a samara, twisted at maturity, about 4 cm (1.5 inches) long, and reddish brown.

Height: Tree of heaven grows from 18 to 25 m (60–80 feet) tall. It has trunk diameters that are usually small, while many trees can be spaced close together.

Range: Tree of heaven is native to China and Taiwan. It has become naturalized throughout most of the United States except the north-central states like Montana and North Dakota. It occurs throughout Washington, Oregon, and California except the driest deserts and semideserts.

Habitat: It is a very invasive tree that is most common along waterways, riparian, valley, and foothill communities on the West Coast and occurs from 0 to 2,000 m (0–6,600 feet). It is very tolerant of disturbed urban sites.

Associated Species: Common associates include Fremont cottonwood, California sycamore, black cottonwood, and red alder.

Similar Trees: Other species, including landscaping trees, with similar compound leaves include Pistache (*Pistacia* spp.), ash, walnut, and pecan. All these trees have a distinctly different type of fruit. Ashes have opposite leaves. Leaves of tree of heaven have a distinct scent that differs from other trees.

Tree Risk Hazard Assessment

Biotic and Abiotic Factors: There are few factors that can cause mortality of tree of heaven, including insects and diseases such as verticillium wilt and spotted lanternfly (*Lycorma delicatula*).

Tree of heaven in disturbed area

Bark

Samara fruit

Leaf

WHITE ALDER
Alnus rhombifolia

Look For: For quick identification, look for a tree with a rounded crown and single stem, usually singly serrated leaves in an uneven pattern, pale white bark that is checkered with age, growing adjacent to streams, conelike fruits, and leafless in the winter months.

Bark: The trunk is pale gray and smooth on young trees, becoming somewhat scaly and checkered with age.

Leaves: The leaves are alternate, ovate to narrow elliptic, 4–10 cm (1.6–4 inches) long, with a singly serrated margin, possibly mixed with small lobes, and a rounded to acute apex; they are thinly hairy below.

Fruit: The male catkins are yellowish, pendulous, slender, 3–10 cm (1.2–4 inches) long. The female catkins are ovoid, 11–22 mm (0.5–0.9 inch) long, resembling a small conifer cone.

Height: It commonly grows 15–25 m (50–80 feet) tall, occasionally up to 30 m (95 feet) tall. It has trunk diameters of usually 25 cm (10 inches), occasionally up to 50 cm (20 inches) wide.

Range: White alder occurs in the western United States in west-central Idaho, Washington, Oregon, and California. This includes the Columbia-Snake River basin, Willamette Valley, southwestern Oregon, and throughout California.

Habitat: It grows along permanent streams in riparian zones from 100 to 2,400 m (330–7,900 feet).

Associated Species: It is commonly associated with trees like big-leaf maple, Oregon ash, sycamore, Fremont cottonwood, black cottonwood, valley oak, willows, and conifers like Douglas fir or incense cedar.

Similar Trees: Other trees with similar leaf shape are red alder, mountain alder, and Sitka alder. Red alder is a tree with doubly serrate leaf margins, and the bark tends to stay smooth with age. Red alder does not occur in Southern California. Mountain alder is a short tree with doubly serrate leaves. Paper birch has a more elongated pointed leaf tip and grows to the north of white alder. There are several small cherry (Prunus) trees on the Pacific coast. Cherry trees have single serrate leaves in an even pattern, a drupe fruit, and usually lenticelled bark.

White alder in riparian area

Bark

Fruit

Leaves

Tree Risk Hazard Assessment

Biotic and Abiotic Factors: There are several factors that can cause mortality of white alder, including insects and diseases such as armillaria root disease, Phellinus trunk rot, invasive shot-hole borer, and flatheaded borer. Other signs that indicate a live tree may have high failure potential include one or more conks on the main stem from trunk rot. Since alders are streamside trees, roots loosened by water can increase failure potential.

RED ALDER
Alnus rubra

Look For: For quick identification, look for a tree with a rounded crown and single stem, pale mottled bark, usually double-serrated leaves with revolute edges, conelike fruits, growing adjacent to streams, and leafless in the winter months.

Bark: The trunk is mottled with shades of white and gray and smooth.

Leaves: The leaves are alternate, ovate, 7–15 cm (3–6 inches) long, double-serrated along the margin and an acute apex. The leaf margins are narrowly revolute, curved under.

Fruit: The male catkins are yellowish, pendulous, slender, 10–15 cm (4–6 inches) long. The female catkins are ovoid, 20–30 mm (0.8–1.2 inches) long, resembling a small conifer cone.

Height: It commonly grows 24–30 m (80–100 feet) tall, occasionally up to 35 m (110 feet) tall. It has trunk diameters of 35–45 cm (14–18 inches), occasionally up to 1 m (3.5 feet) wide.

Range: Red alder occurs from southeastern Alaska along the coast through British Columbia, Washington, Oregon, to central coastal California. This includes the immediate coast and coastal mountain ranges of those states. There are also small populations growing along streams in northern Idaho.

Habitat: It grows along permanent streams in riparian zones, the coastal forest, and moist cool slopes in Douglas fir–hemlock–cedar forest from 0 to 760 m (0–2,500 feet).

Associated Species: It is commonly associated with trees like big-leaf maple, Oregon ash, black cottonwood, willows, and conifers like Douglas fir, Sitka spruce, western hemlock, western red cedar, grand fir, and redwood.

Similar Trees: Other trees with similar leaf shape are white alder, mountain alder, and paper birch. White alder is a tree with single-serrate leaf margins, compared to red alder with double-serrate leaf margins. White alder is usually offset from the Oregon and Washington coastline. Mountain alder is a small tree without strongly revolute leaves. Paper birch has more pointed leaf tips and peeling bark. There are several small cherry (Prunus) trees on the Pacific coast. Cherry trees have single-serrate leaves in an even pattern, a drupe fruit, and usually lenticelled bark.

Red alder in recently disturbed riparian area

Bark

Fruit

Leaves

Tree Risk Hazard Assessment

Biotic and Abiotic Factors: There are several factors that can cause mortality of red alder, including diseases such as armillaria root disease, Phellinus trunk rot, and sapwood rots. Other signs that indicate a live tree may have high failure potential include one or more conks on the main stem (Phellinus trunk rot). Since alders are streamside trees, roots loosened by water can increase failure potential.

PACIFIC MADRONE
Arbutus menziesii

Look For: For quick identification, look for a tree that has partially peeled bark with reddish color on the interior stem and an asymmetric rounded crown, alternate, evergreen, ovate-oblong leaves with mostly smooth margins (occasionally serrate), and a reddish-colored fruit at maturity.

Bark: The trunk is dark brownish red and somewhat flaky and checkered before the bark peels off, revealing a smooth reddish color, and when further peeling turns a light tan brown.

Leaves: The leaves are shiny dark green on top and lighter green on bottom, alternate, evergreen, ovate to oblong, 7–15 cm (3–6 inches) long, smooth edged.

Fruit: Flowers are urn shaped and whitish. The fruit is a round and reddish berry at maturity, 1 cm (0.4 inch).

Height: It commonly grows from 5 to 25 m (16–80 feet) and occasionally up to 40 m (130 feet) tall. It has trunk diameters from 50 to 100 cm (2–3 feet) and up to 2 m (6 feet).

Range: Pacific madrone occurs from southwestern British Columbia south through western Washington, western Oregon, and coastal California to Southern California. It also occurs in the northern Sierra Nevada.

Habitat: It grows in mixed evergreen, oak woodlands, Douglas fir–hemlock–cedar forests from 0 to 1,500 m (0–5,000 feet).

Associated Species: It is commonly associated with hardwoods like canyon live oak, coast live oak, interior live oak, Oregon white oak, California bay, big-leaf maple, tan oak, black oak, and conifers like redwood, Douglas fir, western hemlock, ponderosa pine, and shore pine.

Similar Trees: No other trees native to the West Coast are similar to madrone. California bay has more lanceolate leaves with a grayish trunk that has vertical cracking and fissures. Manzanita shrubs (*Arctostaphylos* spp.) can also reveal a smooth reddish color on the stems but have different leaves and shorter stature. Eucalyptus trees have a different color on the exposed stems and the leaves are different.

Pacific madrone along a saltwater inlet

Stem partially covered with bark

Fruit

Leaves

Tree Risk Hazard Assessment

Biotic and Abiotic Factors: There are several factors that can cause mortality of Pacific madrone, diseases such as annosus root rot, sudden oak death, Arbutus canker, madrone canker, and crown canker. Other signs that indicate a live tree may have failure potential include extensive stem decay.

PAPER BIRCH
Betula papyrifera

Look For: For quick identification, look for a tree with a rounded crown and single stem, copper-colored (usually younger trees) to white bark that is peeling, double-serrated pointed leaves, leafless with cone and catkin-like fruits in the winter months.

Bark: The trunk is white and peeling, occasionally with copper or bronze coloring on the bark of younger trees.

Leaves: The leaves are alternate, dark green, oval to triangular, 4–10 cm (2–4 inches) long, somewhat short hairy, with double serrations along the margin and a tapered pointed tip.

Fruit: The male catkins are yellowish, pendulous, slender, 5–10 cm (2–4 inches) long. The female catkins are ovoid and about 3.5 cm (1.5 inches) long, somewhat resembling a small conifer cone that disintegrates when dried out.

Height: It commonly grows 20–25 m (70–80 feet) tall, occasionally up to 35 m (115 feet) tall. It has trunk diameters of 25–30 cm (10–12 inches), occasionally up to 75 cm (2.5 feet) wide.

Range: Paper birch occurs in a small part of Alaska, most of Canada, and several northern to northeastern states in the contiguous United States.

Habitat: It grows in subboreal spruce hardwood, Douglas fir, lodgepole pine, boreal zones, and swampy areas from sea level to moderate elevations. In southern Alaska, it can grow along the coast.

Associated Species: It is commonly associated with trees like mountain hemlock, subalpine fir, lodgepole pine, Douglas fir, western hemlock, western red cedar, black spruce, white spruce, black cottonwood, balsam polar, and quaking aspen.

Similar Trees: Other trees with similar leaf shape are red alder and other birches. Red alder has white mottled bark that is not peeling, and it is more coastal than paper birch. Water birch is a smaller tree-shrub with shorter leaves, the bark is not readily peeling, and it usually occurs in a wet habitat. Some authors have split *Betula papyrifera* into several species including Kenai birch and resin birch. Kenai birch (*Betula kenaica*) has shorter leaves and occurs in Alaska, while resin or paper birch (*Betula neoalaskana*) is very similar to *Betula papyrifera*, has slight differences in fruiting structures and leaf hairiness,

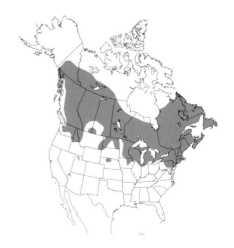

Paper birch in hardwood-conifer mix

Bark

Fruit

Leaves

and occurs more north in the boreal zone of Alaska and northern British Columbia, and northern Canada. There are several small cherry (Prunus) trees on the Pacific coast. Cherry trees have single-serrate leaves, a drupe fruit, and usually lenticelled bark. Paper birch hybridizes with water birch.

Tree Risk Hazard Assessment

Biotic and Abiotic Factors: There are several factors that can cause mortality of paper birch, including insects and diseases such as armillaria root disease, bronze birch borer, and Phellinus trunk rot. Other signs that indicate a live tree may have high failure potential include one or more conks on the main stem of Phellinus trunk rot, white spongy trunk rot, and sterile trunk rot. Paper birch is highly susceptible to fires.

INCENSE CEDAR
Calocedrus decurrens

Look For: For quick identification, look for a conical crown, orange-brown fibrous bark, alternating lengths of leaf scales, somewhat flattened branches, and cone scales that are basally attached and spread apart at maturity.

Bark: The trunk is orange-brown, fibrous, in vertical fissures.

Scalelike Leaves: The leaf scales are 5–15 mm (0.1–0.5 inch) long, alternating length, and arranged in opposite pairs. The leaf branches are somewhat flattened.

Cones: The seed cones are 20–35 mm (0.9–1.4 inches) long, light red-brown, oblong when closed, composed of usually 6 scales. The cone scales separate and reflex upon maturity.

Height: It commonly grows 40–60 m (130–195 feet) tall, occasionally up to 70 m (225 feet) tall. It has trunk diameters up to 4 m (13 feet) wide.

Range: Incense cedar occurs from the mountains in central Oregon south through California to Baja California in Mexico. This includes the Cascades, coast ranges, Sierra Nevada, and mountains of Southern California. It is uncommon in low-elevation forests near the Pacific Ocean and the upper subalpine forests near timberline.

Habitat: It grows on serpentine and non-serpentine soils in mixed conifer, mixed evergreen, Douglas fir–hemlock–cedar (southwestern Oregon), and yellow pine forests at 350–2,500 m (1,100–8,200 feet).

Associated Species: It is commonly associated with trees like Douglas fir, white fir, sugar pine, ponderosa pine, Jeffrey pine, giant sequoia (southern Sierra Nevada), Coulter pine (Southern California), and hardwoods like black oak, canyon live oak, tan oak, California bay, and white alder.

Similar Trees: Other similar conifers with scale-like needles include other cedars, cypresses, junipers, and giant sequoia. Junipers have berry cones. Cypresses, Alaska yellow cedar, and Port Orford cedar have spheric cones that stay spherical when open. Western red cedar has cones similar to incense cedar, but the leaf scales are shorter and consistent in length. Giant sequoia leaf scales are awl-like at the tips and their cones are oblong, staying closed at maturity. The crushed leaves of incense cedar have a distinct scent that is different from other conifer species.

Incense cedar in mixed conifer forest

Bark

Cones

Scalelike leaves

Tree Risk Hazard Assessment

Biotic and Abiotic Factors: Incense cedar has resistance to many biotic factors, but Heterobasidion root disease and occasionally cedar bark beetles can cause tree mortality. Other signs that indicate a tree or branches may have possible failure potential include one or more conks on the main stem from pocket dry rot (*Oligoporus amarus*); however, those trees tend to remain structurally sound. Forked tops can break under pressure of snow and ice. Dead trees can stand for several years.

PORT ORFORD CEDAR
Chamaecyparis lawsoniana

Look For: For quick identification, look for a conical crown, mildly drooping crown and branches, somewhat flattened branches with pronounced X patterns of white stomata, small spherical cones with peltate scales, and fibrous bark.

Bark: The trunk is fibrous, grayish brown with purple and silver shading, and peels in vertical strips.

Scalelike Leaves: The leaves are scalelike, in somewhat flattened branches, yellow green to blue green, and 3–5 mm (0.125 inch) long. The undersides of the branches have X-marked lines of white stomata.

Cones: The cones are greenish maturing to brown, spheric, composed of 6–10 peltate scales, and 14–16 mm (0.6 inch) diameter.

Height: It commonly grows 20–60 m (70–200 feet) tall, occasionally up to 70 m (230 feet) tall. It has trunk diameters from 0.3–2 m (1–6 feet), occasionally up to 3 m (10 feet) wide.

Range: Port Orford cedar occurs in southwestern Oregon and northwestern California along the coast and in the mountains.

Habitat: It grows in redwood, mixed evergreen, mixed conifer, true fir, coastal, and Douglas fir–hemlock–cedar forests from 0 to 1,900 m (0–6,200 feet). It frequently occurs on serpentine and wet soils.

Associated Species: It is commonly associated with trees like Douglas fir, western hemlock, western red cedar, Sitka spruce, western white pine, lodgepole pine, incense cedar, Shasta red fir, white fir, sugar pine, grand fir, and hardwoods like tan oak, California bay, red alder, madrone, and canyon live oak.

Similar Trees: Other cedars, cypresses, and junipers can all appear similar due to their scalelike needles. Juniper trees have berry cones and rounded branches and occur in drier habitats. The cypresses of California have similar cones, but they have rounded branches and occur in drier habitats (except locally landscaped Monterey cypress). Western red cedar has more of a reddish-brown bark and different-type cones. Incense cedar has more flattened branches, longer internode scales, and different-type cones. Alaska yellow cedar has similar slightly flattened branches, but the underside of the branches do not have pronounced X-shaped lines of white stomata. The crushed scales of Port Orford cedar have a distinct scent that differs from that of other cedars, cypresses, and junipers.

Port Orford cedar in mixed conifer forest

Bark

Cones

Scalelike leaves

Tree Risk Hazard Assessment

Biotic and Abiotic Factors: Port Orford cedar has resistance to many biotic factors, but Port Orford cedar root disease (*Phytophthora lateralis*) is highly fatal and is the cause of significant changes in populations of the species. Planting the tree north of its native range can cause death by cold damage. Other signs that indicate that a live tree may have failure potential include heavy winds to root disease–damaged trees. Dead trees without root disease may stand for several years.

ALASKA YELLOW CEDAR
Chamaecyparis nootkatensis

Look For: For quick identification, look for a conical crown, drooping crown and branches, somewhat flattened branches, small spherical cones with peltate scales, fibrous bark, and normally occurring in subalpine zones.

Bark: The trunk is fibrous, irregularly fissured, grayish-white, and peeling.

Scalelike Leaves: The leaves are scalelike, in nearly round branches, and 3–5 mm (0.125 inch) long. The top of the tree and branches are often drooping.

Cones: The cones are greenish to ashy gray, spheric, composed of 4–6 peltate scales, and 11–13 mm (0.5 inch) in diameter.

Height: It commonly grows 20–30 m (65–100 feet) tall, occasionally up to 40 m (130 feet) tall. It has trunk diameters from 60 to 90 cm (2–3 feet), occasionally up to 3.7 m (12 feet) wide.

Range: Alaska yellow cedar (also called *Callitropsis nootkatensis*) occurs from southeastern Alaska through western British Columbia, Washington, and Oregon to northwestern California. This includes the coast ranges, Cascades, and northwestern California mountains. There are isolated occurrences in southeastern British Columbia and central Oregon.

Habitat: It grows in coastal (southeastern Alaska), Douglas fir–hemlock–cedar (British Columbia), true fir, and subalpine forests from 0 to 910 m (0–3,000 feet) in the northern part of its range and 600–2,300 m (2,000–7,500 feet) in the southern part of its range.

Associated Species: It is commonly associated with trees like noble fir, Pacific silver fir, western hemlock, western red cedar, Douglas fir, mountain hemlock, Sitka spruce, and western white pine in most of its range, and incense cedar, Shasta red fir, white fir, Brewer spruce (northwestern California), sugar pine, and Jeffrey pine in the southern part of its range.

Similar Trees: Other cedars, cypresses, and junipers can all appear similar due to their scalelike needles. Juniper trees have berry cones and rounded branches and occur in drier habitats. The cypresses of California have similar cones but with 6–12 scales, have rounded branches, and usually occur in drier habitats. Western red cedar has more of a reddish-brown bark, less drooping branches, different-type cones, and usually occur at lower elevations. Incense cedar has more flattened branches, different-type cones, and usually occur at lower elevations. Port Orford cedar has similar branches,

Bark

Two Alaska yellow cedars in true fir forest

Cones and scalelike leaves

but the underside of the branches has more pronounced X-shaped lines of white stomata, and they also normally occur at lower elevations. The crushed scaly branches of Alaska yellow cedar have a distinct scent that is somewhat similar to Port Orford cedar but differs from that of other cedars, cypresses, and junipers.

Tree Risk Hazard Assessment

Biotic and Abiotic Factors: Alaska yellow cedar has resistance to many biotic factors; nothing appears to be major. Alaska yellow cedar is highly susceptible to fires. Alaska yellow cedar decline in southeastern Alaska is possibly an environmental issue causing tree mortality.

MONTEREY CYPRESS AND OTHERS
Cupressus macrocarpa

Look For: For quick identification of cypresses in general, look for globose cones with peltate scales that have minute or large appendages. The branches on the cypresses are rounded and the scales can have resin glands or not. Cypresses can have fibrous or scaly, peeling bark. Monterey cypress usually has slightly larger cones than the other native cypresses and a more flattened tree crown top.

Bark: The trunk is fibrous and grayish brown.

Scalelike Leaves: The leaf scales are 2–5 mm (0.8–0.2 inch) long on rounded branches. The leaf scales of Monterey cypress are usually without glands and non-resinous.

Cones: The globose cones of Monterey cypress are 25–40 mm (1–1.5 inches), brown, with small appendages on the peltate scales.

Height: Monterey cypress grows to 18–25 m (60–82 feet) tall and has reached 40+ m (130 feet) in other countries. It has trunk diameters from 1+ m (3+ feet), occasionally up to 2.5 m (8 feet) wide.

Range: The cypresses on the West Coast occur mainly in California in a diversity of habitats and geographic locations, but usually with small native ranges. Monterey cypress may have the smallest native range of all the West Coast cypresses, but it is artificially planted and has become naturalized along the coast from California to Oregon. Monterey cypress has a native range in Monterey County, California, in a few locations along the coast.

Habitat: It occurs in coastal habitats from 5 to 35 m (15–115 feet) in its native range.

Associated Species: Associates include mainly Monterey pine and Gowen cypress. It may also occur with bishop pine, lodgepole (shore) pine, Sitka spruce, red alder, redwood, and with coastal grasses.

Similar Trees: Other trees with similar scales are the cedars, junipers, and cypresses. Western red cedar and incense cedar have different cones and more-flattened branches. Port Orford cedar has slightly flattened branches with lines of white stomata on the undersides of the branches. Junipers have berry-like cones. MacNab cypress occurs in chaparral communities surrounding the Sacramento Valley, grows 10–15 m (33–50 feet) tall, and has resinous glands. Baker cypress occurs in juniper woodlands and mixed conifer forest in north-central to northeastern California, grows 10–30 m (33–100 feet) tall, and has resinous

native range
naturalized-planted range

Several Monterey cypresses in coastal grassland

Bark of Monterey cypress

Cones and scalelike leaves of Monterey cypress

glands. Sargent cypress occurs in chaparral in the central coast ranges, grows 5–20 m (16–65 feet) tall, and usually does not have resinous glands. *Cupressus arizonica*, or Cuyamaca and Piute cypress, occurs in pinyon juniper and chaparral in Kern and San Diego Counties, grows to 5–20 m (16–65 feet) tall, and usually has resinous glands. *Cupressus goveniana*, or Gowen, Mendocino, and Santa Cruz cypresses, occurs in coastal, coastal chaparral, or redwood communities.

They grow to 1–20 m (3–65 feet) tall and do not have resinous glands. Tecate cypress occurs in chaparral in southwestern California, grows to 10 m (33 feet) tall, and does not have resinous glands.

Tree Risk Hazard Assessment

Biotic and Abiotic Factors: Literature states very little about abiotic and biotic factors causing serious tree mortality for cypress trees, but one of the main problems is Coryneum canker, and Monterey cypress is more susceptible than other native cypresses. Other signs that indicate a live tree may have failure potential include extensive stem decay.

Piute cypress in pinyon juniper woodland

Bark of Tecate cypress

Sargent cypress in mixed evergreen forest

Baker cypress in mixed conifer forest USDA FOREST
SERVICE PHOTO BY WILLIAM C. WOODRUFF

Cones of MacNab cypress

BLUE GUM EUCALYPTUS AND OTHERS
Eucalyptus globulus

Look For: For quick identification, especially the species in this report, conical to rounded crown, evergreen, alternate, lanceolate leaves with a distinctive aromatic scent, peeling bark to some degree, small usually globose persistent capsules. Blue gum has larger capsules than the other eucalyptus in this report and is useful for identification.

Bark: The trunk is smooth, cream- to reddish-colored, that shreds and peels in large strips. The outer brownish to reddish bark readily peels off.

Leaves: The leaves of blue gum are aromatic, alternate, lanceolate to curved, waxy gray-blue green, 10–30 cm (4–11 inches) long. Juvenile leaves are shorter, wider, lighter-colored, and ovate.

Fruit: The flowers are white and the fruit of blue gum is a woody capsule 12–25 mm (0.5–1 inch) long.

Height: Blue gum commonly grows 30–55 m (100–180 feet) tall in California, occasionally up to 80 m (260 feet) tall in Australia. It has trunk diameters of 15–50 cm (6–20 inches), occasionally up to 2 m (7 feet) wide.

Range: Blue gum eucalyptus is native to Australia and Tasmania. It has become naturalized in California from Humboldt County south to San Diego County. Blue gum is the most widespread naturally occurring species in California and occurs near the coast and Sacramento–San Joaquin Valleys. Red gum (*Eucalyptus camaldulensis*), sugar gum (*Eucalyptus cladocalyx*), and white ironbark (*Eucalyptus leucoxylon*) have become naturalized in limited extent in Southern California and Arizona. There are numerous other eucalyptus species used for landscaping purposes that are not discussed in this book.

Habitat: It occurs in coastal, oak woodlands, chapparal, and annual grasslands from 0 to 300 m (0–1,000 feet).

Associated Species: Blue gum stands usually occur as monocultures, outcompeting other trees. Eucalyptus develop an allelopathy in the leaves, which inhibits other plants from growing around them. In larger blue gum stands on the central California coast, it occurs with Douglas fir, California bay, and coast live oak.

Similar Trees: Other similar eucalyptus species mentioned in this report all have a distinct scent of their aromatic leaves. The other three eucalyptus here have slight differences in bark texture and color, leaf shape and size, number

Blue gum eucalyptus in disturbed area next to creek

Juvenile leaves, fruit, flowers

Bark

Fruit

Leaves

of flowers and fruits in inflorescence, and fruit shape and size. An example of a eucalyptus that does not have peeling bark is red ironbark (*Eucalyptus sideroxylon*). Some eucalyptus have nearly round leaves. There are several other genera in the Lauraceae family with similar leaves. Look for differences in aromatic leaf scents, bark textures, and leaf shape.

Tree Risk Hazard Assessment

Biotic and Abiotic Factors: There are several factors that can cause mortality of eucalyptus trees, including insects and diseases such as phytophthora root rot and red-gum lerp psyllid. Other signs that indicate a live tree may have high failure potential include extensive decay on the main stem. Frost or cold damage is common for eucalyptus.

OREGON ASH
Fraxinus latifolia

Look For: For quick identification, look for a tree with a rounded-to-spreading crown, usually a single stem, gray furrowed bark, compound leaf with ovate leaflets, straight winged samara fruit, growing in wet areas, and leafless in the winter months.

Bark: The trunk is grayish brown with vertical and diagonal furrows and fissures.

Leaves: The leaves are green, opposite, pinnately compound, 15–30 cm (4–12 inches) long. The 5–7 leaflets are ovate to oblong, 6–12 cm (2–5 inches), smooth to serrate on the margins.

Fruit: The fruit is a straight to slightly curved winged samara, 3–5 cm (1.5–3 inches) long.

Height: It commonly grows 12–24 m (40–80 feet) tall, taller in favorable conditions. It has trunk diameters of 40–75 cm (16–30 inches).

Range: Oregon ash occurs in western Washington, western Oregon, and through most of California. In California this includes the northern coast range, the Sierra Nevada, and Southern California mountains.

Habitat: It grows along streams and in wetlands primarily in riparian forests from 0 to 1,500 m (0–5,000 feet), usually below 900 m (3,000 feet).

Associated Species: It is commonly associated with trees like big-leaf maple, Oregon white oak, red alder, white alder, black cottonwood, willows, interior live oak, California bay, California sycamore, and conifers like Douglas fir, grand fir, incense cedar, and ponderosa pine.

Similar Trees: Other trees with similar leaf shape are other ashes and walnuts. Velvet ash is a shorter tree of Southern California riparian areas and more lanceolate-shaped leaflets. Green ash is naturalized east of the Cascades and has slightly more-lanceolate leaflets. Walnuts are alternate leaved and most have lanceolate leaflets, but California black walnut–English walnut hybrids have ovate leaflets and a nearly spherical hard fruit. Mountain ashes (Sorbus) have narrower leaflets and a different-type fruit. Tree of heaven has more lanceolate-shaped leaflets.

Tree Risk Hazard Assessment

Biotic and Abiotic Factors: Literature states very little about abiotic and biotic factors causing tree mortality for Oregon ash. Oregon ash is reportedly susceptible to the emerald ash borer.

Oregon ash in riparian area

Bark

Fruit

Leaf

Emerald ash borer was found in Oregon in 2022. Landscaping trees such as white and green ash, which are widely planted across the United States, are frequently attacked in other parts of the country by the emerald ash borer. Other signs that indicate a live tree may have high failure potential include one or more conks on the main stem of white mottled rot.

ENGLISH WALNUT
Juglans regia

Look For: For quick identification, look for a tree with a rounded-to-spreading crown, compound leaves that have straight elliptic-to-ovate leaflets, grayish bark that is somewhat smooth to furrowed, and nearly globular hard-shelled nuts.

Bark: The trunk can be somewhat smooth to becoming widely cracked with shallow furrows.

Leaves: The leaves are deciduous, alternate, pinnately compound, green, and 25–40 cm (10–16 inches) long. Each leaf has 5–9 lanceolate-to-elliptic leaflets that are straight, usually entire, and 5–18 cm (2–7 inches) long. The terminal leaflet is usually wider and longer than the lateral leaflets. The twigs have chambered piths.

Fruit: The fruit is a hard-shelled nut, 4–5 cm (1.5 inches), brown, with a skin that turns from green to brown.

Height: It typically grows 15–20 m (40–70 feet) tall and sometimes up to 30 m (100 feet). It has trunk diameters up to 1 m (3 feet) wide.

Range: English walnut is native to southeastern Europe and Asia. It is used commercially in the western United States, especially in California as an orchard tree. It is also used as a landscaping tree and has become naturalized in the wild. Many walnut orchards use hybrid rootstocks, usually *J. hindsii* × *J. regia*.

Habitat: It can be found most commonly in orchards but also riparian areas and abandoned fields.

Associated Species: Other riparian trees like cottonwoods and willows when growing in riparian areas.

Similar Trees: Other species with similar leaves are Oregon ash. Oregon ash has opposite leaves and samara fruits, compared to the hard-shelled nuts of walnut. California black walnut has more leaflets that are serrated and narrower. Another orchard tree, pecan, has narrower leaflets that are curved and a fruit that is more oblong than round.

Tree Risk Hazard Assessment

Biotic and Abiotic Factors: Literature states very little about abiotic and biotic factors causing tree mortality for English walnut. Various forms of root rot can cause mortality. It does not appear to be very susceptible to

English walnut along path in riparian area

Bark

Fruit

Leaf

mortality from thousand cankers disease. Because of its height and fast growth rates, English walnut growing in orchards is a common problem for encroaching upon electric power lines.

WESTERN AND SIERRA JUNIPER
Juniperus occidentalis var. *occidentalis* and *australis*

Look For: For quick identification, look for an asymmetrical or symmetrical conic crown, orange-brown (Sierra juniper) or grayish-brown (western juniper) fibrous bark, round branches, leaf scales with resin, berry-like cones, and usually a single-stemmed tree.

Bark: The trunk is orange brown to gray brown for western juniper and more orange brown for Sierra juniper, fibrous, and peeling vertically.

Scalelike Leaves: The leaf scales are in whorls of 3 or 4, 2–3 mm (0.1 inch) long, and usually have glands with resin. Leaf scale margins are serrated at 20X magnification. The leaf branches are round.

Cone: The berry-like cones are 6–10 mm (0.25–0.4 inch), light blue, and round.

Height: It commonly grows 10–15 m (30–50 feet) tall, occasionally up to 30 m (100 feet) tall. It has trunk diameters of 30–100 cm (1–3.3 feet), and sometimes up to 2.5 m (8 feet) wide.

Range: Western juniper (variety *occidentalis*) occurs from southeastern Washington through central and eastern Oregon, southwestern Idaho, northwestern Nevada, and northwestern California. Sierra juniper (variety *australis*) occurs throughout much of California and west-central Nevada. The range map shows western juniper in the north and Sierra juniper in the south.

Habitat: It grows in pinyon juniper, mixed conifer, yellow pine forests, and up to subalpine at 200–3,050 m (600–10,000 feet). It normally does not occur near the Pacific Ocean in Douglas fir–hemlock–cedar forests.

Associated Species: Western juniper occurs with ponderosa pine and Oregon white oak, or can occur as the only tree and is closely associated with the shrub big sagebrush (*Artemisia* spp.). Sierra juniper occurs with single-leaf pinyon, white fir, Jeffrey pine, red fir, lodgepole pine, and hardwoods like black oak and canyon live oak.

Similar Trees: Other similar conifers with scalelike needles include other junipers, cypresses, and cedars. Cypresses and Port Orford cedar have round cones with peltate scales. Western red cedar and incense cedar have cones with overlapping scales, and the branches are more flattened. Utah juniper is shorter than western-Sierra juniper, and scales are glandless without resin. California juniper occurs in the form of a shrub and lacks resinous leaf scale glands. Rocky Mountain juniper

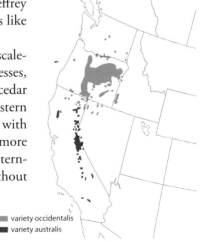

variety occidentalis
variety australis

Sierra juniper with Jeffrey pine and other junipers

Western juniper in juniper woodland

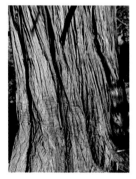

Cone and scalelike leaves

Bark of Sierra juniper

Bark of western juniper

slightly overlaps with western juniper in Oregon and Washington, and it has thin branches and scales that usually lack resin and margins without serrations at 20X magnification. The crushed scales and branches of juniper have a distinct scent.

Tree Risk Hazard Assessment

Biotic and Abiotic Factors: There are a few factors that can cause mortality of western and Sierra juniper, including insects and diseases such as root rot and juniper bark beetle. Dead trees can stand for several years.

WESTERN LARCH
Larix occidentalis

Look For: For quick identification, look for a conical, somewhat symmetrical crown, many needles clustered on short stem pegs, cone scales with one exserted bract, thickly furrowed bark, and without needles in the winter months.

Bark: The trunk on mature trees has thick bark that is orange gray and irregularly deeply furrowed.

Needles: The needles are light green, deciduous, and turning yellow in fall, growing singly toward the branch tips and clustered on short pegs on the older branches, 2–5 cm (0.75–2 inches) long, flexible.

Cone: The cone is pendant, red brown, 2–5 cm (0.75–2 inches) long, with each scale bearing a single bract 4–8 mm long.

Height: It commonly grows 30–55 m (100–180 feet) tall, occasionally over 60 m (200 feet) tall. It has trunk diameters of 0.8–1.5 m (2.5–5 feet), occasionally up to 2 m (6.5 feet) wide.

Range: Western larch occurs from southeastern British Columbia south through central and eastern Washington and Oregon, and east through northern Idaho to northwestern Montana. This includes the Cascades and northern Rocky Mountains.

Habitat: It grows in lower subalpine, lodgepole pine, ponderosa pine, Douglas fir–grand fir forests, at 600–2,200 m (2,000–7,200 feet). It is rare in western Cascade forests like true fir or Pacific silver fir.

Associated Species: It is commonly associated with trees like Douglas fir, subalpine fir, ponderosa pine, western hemlock, western red cedar, Engelmann spruce, grand fir, lodgepole pine, and western white pine.

Similar Trees: Other trees with similar needles are the other larches. Subalpine larch grows at higher elevations and has slightly longer cones and more hair on the twigs. Tamarack grows in boreal bogs far to the north and has glabrous twigs.

Tree Risk Hazard Assessment

Biotic and Abiotic Factors: There are a few factors that can cause mortality of western larch, including insects and diseases such as dwarf mistletoe (*Arceuthobium laricis*) and spruce budworm. Other signs that indicate a live tree may have high failure potential include one or more conks on the main stem (schweinitzii butt rot, brown trunk rot).

Western larch with lodgepole pine forest

Bark

Cone

Needles

TAN OAK
Lithocarpus densiflorus

Look For: For quick identification, look for a tree with a rounded-to-spreading crown, that has alternate, evergreen leaves with toothed margins and a white hairy lower surface. The acorns have appendages, and bark on mature trees has an irregular pattern.

Bark: The trunk is gray and can be somewhat smooth, with irregular cracks, or somewhat blocky with ridges.

Leaves: The leaves are shiny light to dark green on top and convex, alternate, evergreen, and hairy to whitish beneath, oblong, 7–15 cm (3–6 inches) long, usually toothed. The leaf veins can appear to be indented on top.

Fruit: The acorn nut is 20–30 mm (0.8–1.2 inches) long, and the acorn cap has numerous short bristles.

Height: It commonly grows to 20–25 m (65–80 feet) and occasionally up to 40 m (130 feet) tall. It has trunk diameters of 20–80 cm (0.5–2.5 feet) and up to 2 m (6 feet).

Range: Tan oak (also called *Notholithocarpus densiflorus*) occurs from southwestern Oregon south through the northern and central California coast ranges. It also occurs in the northern Sierra Nevada.

Habitat: It grows in mixed evergreen and redwood forests from 40 to 1,500 m (150–5,000 feet).

Associated Species: It is commonly associated with hardwoods like canyon live oak, coast live oak, black oak, Oregon white oak, big-leaf maple, California bay, Pacific madrone, red alder, and conifers like redwood Douglas fir, Port Orford cedar, knobcone pine, western hemlock, and incense cedar.

Similar Trees: Other trees with similar leaves are coast live oak, canyon live oak, Shreve oak, and interior live oak. Shreve oak and interior live oak have shiny lower leaf surfaces. Canyon live oak can be very similar and has golden hairy dull or whitish leaf surfaces and the leaves are not convex. Canyon live oak does not have indented veins on tops of the leaves. Coast live oak has convex leaves, but the lower surface is glabrous not hairy. Giant chinquapin can have very similar leaves, but they tend to be narrower, smooth margined, and a more permanent golden color on the undersides. Island oak leaves are similar; however, those trees occur on the Channel Islands in California. The oaks in Quercus lack the acorn cap appendages.

Two tan oak in mixed evergreen forest

Bark

Bark

Fruit

Leaves

Tree Risk Hazard Assessment

Biotic and Abiotic Factors: There are a few factors that could cause a tan oak to die. Several insects and diseases can contribute to mortality, including armillaria root disease and sudden oak death disease. Sudden oak death disease has killed millions of tan oak in its range near the Pacific coast. Other signs that indicate a live tree may have high failure potential include one-third of the stem decayed with sudden oak death disease.

ENGELMANN SPRUCE
Picea engelmannii

Look For: For quick identification, look for conical, symmetrical, occasionally spire-shaped crown, 4-sided sharp pointed needles, short hairy twigs, short pendant cones with jagged scale tips, and scaly bark.

Bark: The trunk is grayish to reddish brown, thin and scaly, peeling in circular plates.

Needles: The needles are 4-sided, blue green, stiff, sharp pointed, and 2–3 cm (0.8–1.2 inches) long.

Cones: The cone is light brown, pendant, and 4–8 cm (1.5–3.5 inches) long with jagged cone-scale margins.

Height: It commonly grows 15–40 m (50–130 feet) tall, occasionally up to 65 m (215 feet) tall. It has trunk diameters of 40–75 cm (15–30 inches), occasionally up to 2 m (6.5 feet) wide.

Range: Engelmann spruce occurs from British Columbia south through Washington, and in Oregon to northwestern California. It occurs east to western Alberta through the Rockies to New Mexico and northern Mexico.

Habitat: Along the Pacific coast, it grows in subboreal white spruce hardwood (British Columbia), Douglas fir–grand fir, lodgepole pine, true fir, subalpine forests, and riparian zones from 600 to 2,400 m (2,000–8,000 feet). It is not common in drier forests with ponderosa pine.

Associated Species: It is commonly associated with trees like subalpine fir, whitebark pine, Pacific silver fir, alpine larch, grand fir, Douglas fir, mountain hemlock, lodgepole pine, and western white pine in most of its range; white spruce, balsam poplar, and paper birch in the northern part of its range; and additionally, Shasta red fir, Brewer spruce, incense cedar, and sugar pine in the southern part of its range.

Similar Trees: Other trees with similar needles include spruces and Douglas fir. Sitka spruce has 2-sided needles that are very sharp at the tip and can puncture skin. White spruce has glabrous twigs and cones with entire scale tips. Black spruce has shorter needles, has shorter cones, and usually occurs in bogs. Brewer spruce has 2-sided needles that are blunt pointed at the tip and with needles not very aromatic. Mountain hemlock has blunt flexible needles but with somewhat similar cones. Douglas fir has flexible, non-sharp pointed needles, and cones with pitchfork bracts extending from

Bark

Cones

Engelmann spruce with other spruces in riparian area

beneath the scales in the cone. Engelmann spruce hybridizes with white spruce in central British Columbia. The crushed needles of Engelmann spruce have a distinct scent that differs from that of other genuses.

Tree Risk Hazard Assessment

Biotic and Abiotic Factors: There are a few factors that can cause mortality of Engelmann spruce, including insects and diseases such as tomentosus root disease, spruce beetle, and

Needles

western spruce budworm. Engelmann spruce is very susceptible to fires. Other signs that indicate a live tree may have failure potential are from tomentosus root disease decay.

WHITE SPRUCE AND HYBRIDS
Picea glauca and hybrids (Picea X albertiana, Picea X lutzii)

Look For: For quick identification, look for conical symmetrical-shaped crown, 3- or 4-sided sharp pointed needles, short pendant cones with wide smooth-edged scale tips, smooth to scaly bark, and glabrous twigs. White spruce hybrids tend to have cones with ragged margins on the scales.

Bark: The trunk is grayish, thin, and somewhat smooth or scaly.

Needles: The needles are 3- or 4-sided, blue green, stiff, sharp pointed, and 1.5–2 cm (0.6–0.8 inch) long. The twigs are glabrous.

Cones: The cone is light brown, pendant, fan-shaped entire scales (can be diamond shaped with erose tips in hybrids), and 3–7 cm (1.2–2.8 inches) long.

Height: It commonly grows 15–30 m (50–100 feet) tall, occasionally up to 55 m (180 feet) tall. It has trunk diameters up to 60–90 cm (2–3 feet) wide.

Range: White spruce occurs in Alaska, most of Canada, and several northern states in the contiguous United States.

Habitat: It grows in subboreal spruce hardwood, boreal, subalpine, and riparian zones from 0 to 2,000 m (0–7,000 feet). Hybrids also occur in the coastal and lodgepole pine types.

Associated Species: It is commonly associated with trees like subalpine fir, mountain hemlock, lodgepole pine, Douglas fir, black spruce, Sitka spruce, Engelmann spruce, black cottonwood, balsam polar, paper birch, and quaking aspen.

Similar Trees: Other trees with similar needles include Sitka spruce, Engelmann spruce, black spruce, mountain hemlock, and Douglas fir. Sitka spruce has 2-sided needles that are very sharp at the tip and can puncture skin. Engelmann spruce has short bristly hairy twigs. Black spruce has shorter needles and short hairy twigs. Mountain hemlock has blunt flexible needles but with somewhat similar cones. Douglas fir has flexible, non-sharp pointed needles and cones with pitchfork bracts extending from beneath the scales in the cone. White spruce hybridizes with Sitka spruce (*X lutzii*) and with Engelmann spruce (*X albertiana*). The hybrids can have characteristics of both species contributing. White spruce needles have a slightly different scent from other spruces.

Several white spruce with hardwoods in subboreal forest

Bark

Cones

Needles

Tree Risk Hazard Assessment

Biotic and Abiotic Factors: There are several factors that can cause mortality of white spruce, including insects and diseases such as tomentosus root disease, spruce beetle, and eastern spruce budworm. White spruce is highly susceptible to fires.

BLACK SPRUCE
Picea mariana

Look For: For quick identification, look for symmetrical, possible spire-shaped crown, 3- or 4-sided sharp pointed short needles, short pendant cones, scaly bark, hairy twigs, and often growing in muskegs or sphagnum bogs alone or with tamarack.

Bark: The trunk is grayish, thin, and scaly.

Needles: The needles are 3- or 4-sided, blue green, stiff, blunt pointed, and 0.6–1.5 cm (0.25–0.6 inch) long. The twigs are bristly hairy.

Cones: The cone is light brown, pendant, and 1.5–3.5 cm (0.6–1.4 inches) long, with fan-shaped entire scales.

Height: It commonly grows 9–15 m (30–50 feet) tall, occasionally up to 25 m (80 feet) tall. It has trunk diameters of 15–25 cm (6–10 inches) wide.

Range: Black spruce occurs in Alaska, most of Canada, and several northeastern states in the contiguous United States.

Habitat: It grows in subboreal spruce hardwood, boreal, and wetlands (moss or sphagnum bogs) from 0 to 1,000 m (0–3,200 feet). It usually forms a mosaic of black spruce bogs and white spruce hardwoods in the landscape.

Associated Species: It is commonly associated with trees like white spruce, tamarack, subalpine fir, lodgepole pine, balsam polar, paper birch, and quaking aspen.

Similar Trees: Other trees with similar needles include Sitka spruce, Engelmann spruce, white spruce, and mountain hemlock. Sitka spruce has 2-sided needles that are very sharp at the tip and can puncture skin. Engelmann spruce has longer needles and cones with erose tipped scales. White spruce has longer needles and glabrous twigs. Mountain hemlock has blunt flexible needles but with somewhat similar cones. Black spruce has needles that are scented slightly different from other spruces.

Tree Risk Hazard Assessment

Biotic and Abiotic Factors: There are a few factors that can cause mortality of black spruce in the western part of its range including diseases such as tomentosus root disease and possibly eastern spruce budworm. Black spruce is highly susceptible to fires.

Numerous black spruce trees in black spruce bog

Bark

Cones

Needles

SITKA SPRUCE
Picea sitchensis

Look For: For quick identification, look for conical symmetrical crown, tall trees along coastline (along coastal rivers also), 2-sided very sharp pointed needles, glabrous twigs, short pendant cones with jagged scales tips, and scaly bark.

Bark: The trunk is grayish to purplish brown, thin and scaly, peeling in circular plates. Some of the larger trees, especially farther north, have bark with rectangular plates in the lower trunk.

Needles: The needles are 2-sided, blue green, sharp, can puncture skin, and 15–25 mm (0.6–1 inch) long. The twigs are glabrous.

Cones: The cone is light brown, pendant, jagged on the scale tips, and 5–10 cm (2–4 inches) long.

Height: It grows to 70 m (230 feet) tall, occasionally up to 90 m (300 feet) tall. It has trunk diameters from 1.5 to 2 m (5–6.5 feet), occasionally up to 5 m (16 feet) wide.

Range: Sitka spruce occurs from south-central and southeastern Alaska, through western British Columbia, Washington, and Oregon to northwestern California. This includes the coast ranges and western Cascades.

Habitat: It grows in coastal and Douglas fir–hemlock–cedar forests from 0 to 900 m (3,000 feet) in the northern part of its range and in coastal forest from 0 to 400 m (0–1,300 feet) in the southern part of its range. It reaches subalpine forests in Alaska, but not Washington, Oregon, or California.

Associated Species: It is commonly associated with trees like white spruce (southern Alaska), mountain hemlock, Alaska yellow cedar, lodgepole pine, western white pine, grand fir, red alder, western hemlock, Douglas fir, western red cedar, and redwood (southern part of its range).

Similar Trees: Other trees with similar needles include the spruces and Douglas fir. Engelmann spruce has 4-sided needles that are sharp pointed, but not needle-like sharp. Brewer spruce has 2-sided needles that are blunt pointed at the tip and with crushed needles not very aromatic. White spruce has 3- or 4-sided needles with entire fan-shaped scales. Black spruce has shorter needles and hairy twigs. Douglas fir has flexible, non-sharp pointed needles and cones with pitchfork bracts extending from beneath the scales in the cone. Sitka spruce hybridizes with white spruce in south-central Alaska.

Sitka spruce with western hemlocks and other spruces in coastal forest

Bark

Cones

Needles

The crushed needles of Sitka spruce have a distinct scent that differs from that of other genuses.

Tree Risk Hazard Assessment

Biotic and Abiotic Factors: There are a few factors that cause mortality of Sitka spruce, including diseases such as armillaria root disease and the spruce beetle. Sitka spruce stands can be flattened by strong coastal windstorms. Other signs that indicate a live tree may have high failure potential include one or more conks on the main stem (schweinitzii butt rot).

WHITEBARK PINE
Pinus albicaulis

Look For: For quick identification, look for an asymmetrical or symmetrical rounded crown, purple symmetrical cones that fall apart while on the tree, grayish bark in irregular rectangular plates, and 5 needles in a bundle that are stiff and slightly curved.

Bark: The bark is smooth on younger trees and on mature trees is gray to gray white, separated into loose scaly plates.

Needles: The needles are yellow green, 5 per bundle, 3–7 cm (1.2–2.8 inches) long, stiff and curved.

Cones: The cone is ovoid and symmetric, purple-brown, 3.5–9 cm (1.3–3.5 inches) long, erect to spreading, and they fall apart on the tree at maturity.

Height: It commonly grows 12–18 m (40–60 feet) tall, occasionally up to 20 m (65 feet) tall. It has trunk diameters of 60–90 cm (2–3 feet), occasionally up to 1.5 m (5 feet) wide.

Range: Whitebark pine occurs from southern British Columbia south through Washington and Oregon, to the southern Sierra Nevada of California. It also occurs from the Pacific Ocean east through Idaho to western Montana and Wyoming. This includes the Olympic Mountains in Washington, the Klamath Mountains, the Cascades, and the northern Rocky Mountains.

Habitat: It grows primarily in subalpine forests, at elevations from 1,700 to 2,600 m (5,700–8,500 feet) in the northern part of its range to 3,050–3,700 m (10,000–12,100 feet) in the southern part of its range.

Associated Species: It is commonly associated with trees like subalpine fir, Engelmann spruce, subalpine larch, red fir, lodgepole pine, limber pine, foxtail pine, western white pine, mountain hemlock, and Douglas fir.

Similar Trees: Other similar 5-needle pines include limber, foxtail, bristlecone, and western white pine. Limber pine has longer cones that turn from green to light brown, are pendant, and do not break apart at maturity. Western white pine has longer cones, slightly longer blue-green flexible needles, and a bark pattern of square type plates. Foxtail and bristlecone pines have cones with short to long prickles on the scales.

Whitebark pine with Shasta red fir and other pines in subalpine forest

Bark

Cones

Needles

Tree Risk Hazard Assessment

Biotic and Abiotic Factors: There are a few factors that can cause mortality of whitebark pine, including insects and diseases such as dwarf mistletoe (*Arceuthobium cyanocarpum*), white pine blister rust, and mountain pine beetle. Other signs that indicate that a live tree may have failure potential include extensive sapwood or heartwood rot.

KNOBCONE PINE
Pinus attenuata

Look For: For quick identification, look for trees with a conical symmetric or asymmetric crown, in chaparral areas or mixed evergreen forest, 3 medium-length needles per bundle, and cones with knobby tips that are whorled in threes to sixes around stems and branches.

Bark: The trunk is grayish brown with flat scaly ridges.

Needles: The needles are blue green, 3 per bundle, 9–15 cm (3.5–6 inches) long.

Cones: The cone is asymmetric, yellow brown, 6–18 cm (2.5–7 inches) long, and they tend to occur in whorls of 3–6 on branches and stems. The cone-scale tip knobs are angled and prickled.

Height: It commonly grows from 8 to 24 m (25–80 feet), occasionally up to 36 m (120 feet) tall. It has trunk diameters of 35–60 cm (13–23 inches), occasionally up to 1.1 m (3.6 feet) wide.

Range: Knobcone pine occurs from the mountains of southern Oregon, through California to Baja California in Mexico.

Habitat: It grows on serpentine or non-serpentine soils in mixed evergreen forest, chaparral, occasionally oak woodlands from 180 to 2,000 m (600–6,500 feet). It is less common in mixed conifer forests. It can also grow in pure stands in chaparral communities.

Associated Species: It is commonly associated with trees like big-cone Douglas fir, Douglas fir, gray pine, sugar pine, shore pine, Monterrey pine, several cypress species, and hardwoods like tan oak, Pacific madrone, canyon live oak, and interior live oak.

Similar Trees: Other similar pines include Monterey, shore, and bishop pine. Shore and bishop pines have 2 needles per bundle. Monterey pine has smaller scale tip knobs and a different bark texture from knobcone pine. Monterey pine usually is grown as an ornamental tree along roads or developed areas. Gray and Coulter pines have larger, thicker cones and longer needles.

Tree Risk Hazard Assessment

Biotic and Abiotic Factors: There are several factors that can cause mortality of knobcone pine, including insects and diseases such as armillaria root disease, pitch canker, California five-spine Ips, and mountain pine beetle. Other signs that

Knobcone pine with shorter Coulter pines in chaparral woodland

Bark

Needles

Cones

indicate a live tree may have failure potential include extensive stem or heart-wood decay. It is not unusual to find standing dead knobcone pine more than a few years after mortality.

LODGEPOLE PINE AND VARIETIES
Pinus contorta **var.**

Look For: For quick identification, look for a conical symmetrical crown, short symmetric or asymmetrical cones, reddish-orange-brown scaly bark (furrowed and grayish on the Pacific coast), and 2 short needles in a bundle.

Bark: The trunk is gray to orange brown and scaly or furrowed. Variety *contorta* along the Pacific coast has furrowed bark that is somewhat checkered. Variety *latifolia* can have scaly or platy bark.

Needles: The needles are yellow green, 2 per bundle, 2.5–8.5 cm (1–3.3 inches) long.

Cones: The cone is pendant, symmetrical or asymmetrical, persistent or non-persistent, yellow brown, 2–6 cm (0.8–2.3 inches) long. Variety *murrayana* has non-persistent cones, while variety *latifolia* has persistent cones that stay on trees for several years.

Height: Lodgepole pine commonly grows from 6 to 35 m (20–115 feet) tall, occasionally up to 50 m (160 feet) tall. It has trunk diameters of 15–50 cm (6–20 inches), occasionally up to 2 m (7 feet) wide.

Range: Lodgepole pine occurs from southeastern Alaska and Yukon, Canada, south through British Columbia, Washington, Oregon, and California to Baja California, Mexico. It occurs along the Pacific Ocean, east to western South Dakota. There are several subspecies on the West Coast and throughout its range. Shore pine (variety *contorta*) occurs primarily at low elevations along the Pacific Ocean (blue on the map) and is the shortest of the varieties. Variety *murrayana* occurs in the Oregon Cascades and the mountains in California (yellow on map). Variety *latifolia* occurs in central and eastern Washington, central British Columbia, and the Rocky Mountains (orange).

This book covers all three varieties occurring on the West Coast.

Habitat: Lodgepole pine occurs in coastal forests, lodgepole pine forests, true fir, subalpine, and sub-boreal white spruce hardwood forests at low to high elevations from 0 to 3,400 m (0–11,200 feet).

Associated Species: In the mountains of California, it is commonly associated with trees like mountain hemlock, red fir, grand juniper, whitebark pine, foxtail pine, western white pine, Jeffrey pine, western juniper, and hardwoods like quaking aspen. In Oregon and Washington it occurs with ponderosa pine, grand fir, western larch, subalpine fir, Engelmann spruce, and Douglas fir. In British Columbia

Lodgepole pine in mixed conifer forest

Bark of lodgepole pine

Needles, closed cones, and opened cone

Bark of shore pine

Cones of shore pine

Shore pine trees in coastal zone

it additionally occurs with white spruce, black cottonwood, balsam polar, and paper birch. On the Pacific Ocean it occurs with Sitka spruce, bishop pine, grand fir, Douglas fir, and western hemlock. It normally does not occur in oak woodlands or mixed evergreen forests.

Similar Trees: Other similar short two-needle pines include bishop pine. Bishop pine has longer cones and they are usually whorled and attached to stems and branches. Knobcone and Monterey pine both have 3 needles per bundle and they also have longer cones that are usually attached and whorled on stems and branches.

Tree Risk Hazard Assessment

Biotic and Abiotic Factors: There are several factors that can cause mortality of lodgepole pine, including insects and diseases such as Heterobasidion and armillaria root disease, dwarf mistletoe, comandra blister rust, western gall rust, Atropellis canker, Ips spp. beetles, and mountain bark beetle. Other signs that indicate that a live tree may have high failure potential include cankers from western gall rust. Lodgepole pine is very sensitive to fires.

COULTER PINE
Pinus coulteri

Look For: For quick identification, look for trees with a conical to rounded crown, in chaparral or bordering forested areas, 3 long needles per bundle, and large, heavy, yellowish-brown cones with reflexed scale tips that are continuous with the cone scales.

Bark: The trunk is grayish brown with irregular furrows.

Needles: The needles are blue green, 3 per bundle, 15–30 cm (6–12 inches) long.

Cones: The cone is pendant, ovoid-oblong, yellow brown, 20–40 cm (8–15 inches) long, and they tend to occur in whorls of up to 4 or can hang singly. The cone scales are elongated with reflexed tips and pointed.

Height: It commonly grows from 10–25 m (35–80 feet) tall, occasionally up to 40 m (140 feet) tall. It has trunk diameters of 30–80 cm (1–2.5 feet), occasionally up to 1 m (3.5 feet) wide.

Range: Coulter pine occurs in the central California coast ranges and Southern California mountains to Baja California in Mexico.

Habitat: It grows in chaparral, mixed evergreen, and mixed conifer from 700–2,000 m (2,300–7,000 feet).

Associated Species: It is commonly associated with trees like big-cone Douglas fir, gray pine, incense cedar, ponderosa pine, knobcone pine, Jeffrey pine, and hardwoods like coast live oak, black oak, canyon live oak, and interior live oak.

Similar Trees: Other similar three-needle pines include gray pine. Gray pine has shorter cones that are darker-brown in color. Gray pine trees are usually not erect. Ponderosa and Jeffrey pine have cones without large reflexed scale tips. Knobcone and Monterey pine have shorter needles and cones that stayed closed while on the tree.

Tree Risk Hazard Assessment

Biotic and Abiotic Factors: There are a few factors that can cause mortality of Coulter pine, including insects and diseases such as armillaria root disease and western bark beetle.

Coulter pine in chaparral woodland

Bark

Cones

Needles

LIMBER PINE
Pinus flexilis

Look For: For quick identification, look for a conical symmetrical crown, short symmetrical cones, grayish bark in irregular rectangular plates, and 5 needles in a bundle that are stiff and slightly curved.

Bark: The trunk on mature trees is dark gray to dark brown, furrowed into irregular rectangular plates.

Needles: The needles are yellow green, 5 per bundle, 3–9 cm (1.2–3.5 inches) long, stiff, and curved.

Cones: The cone is pendant, yellow brown, 7–15 cm (2.75–6 inches) long, without prickles on the scale tips.

Height: It commonly grows 12–15 m (40–50 feet) tall, occasionally up to 25 m (80 feet) tall. It has trunk diameters of 60–90 cm (2–3 feet), occasionally up to 2.5 m (8 feet) wide.

Range: Limber pine occurs in California primarily in the Sierra Nevada, and Transverse and Peninsular ranges of Southern California. It also occurs in the Rockies and Intermountain ranges from southeastern British Columbia and the Wallowa Mountains in northeastern Oregon south to northern Arizona and New Mexico.

Habitat: On the West Coast it grows in subalpine, lodgepole pine forests, occasionally other conifer types, at elevations of 2,200–3,400 m (7,200–11,150 feet).

Associated Species: It is commonly associated with trees like white fir, lodgepole pine, whitebark pine, foxtail pine, Sierra juniper, Jeffrey pine, single-leaf pinyon, bristlecone pine in the White Mountains in California, and Douglas fir and Rocky mountain juniper in the Oregon Wallowas.

Similar Trees: Other similar 5-needle pines include sugar pine and western white pine. Sugar pine and western white pine both have longer cones. Sugar pine has blue-green flexible needles that are twisted. Western white pine has blue-green flexible needles and a bark pattern of square-type plates. Whitebark, foxtail, and bristlecone pine are upper subalpine species with shorter cones. Whitebark pine has cones that break apart before falling to the ground. Foxtail and bristlecone pines have cones with short to long prickles on the scales.

Limber pine with Jeffrey pine in subalpine forest

Bark

Cones

Needles

Tree Risk Hazard Assessment

Biotic and Abiotic Factors: There are several factors that can cause mortality of limber pine, including insects and diseases such as armillaria root disease, dwarf mistletoe (*Arceuthobium cyanocarpum*), white pine blister rust, and mountain pine beetle. Other signs that indicate a live tree may have failure potential include stem or heartwood rot.

JEFFREY PINE
Pinus jeffreyi

Look For: For quick identification, look for a broad symmetrical crown, 3 long needles in a bundle, medium-length symmetrical cones with incurved scale prickles, and reddish-brown bark with vertical plates.

Bark: The trunk is reddish brown and has narrowly spaced deep irregular furrows or widely spaced shallow furrows in vertical rectangular plates. Some authors use the odor of vanilla/lemon/banana in the bark crevices to be an identifying characteristic; however, in my experience it has not been consistent.

Needles: The needles are yellow green, 3 per bundle, 8–28 cm (3–11 inches) long.

Cones: The cone is symmetrical, pendant, ovate, reddish brown, 12–30 cm (5–12 inches) long. The cone-scale tips have prickles pointing up or curving inward.

Height: It commonly grows 25–40 m (80–130 feet) tall, occasionally up to 55 m (175 feet) tall. It has trunk diameters of 60–120 cm (2–4 feet), occasionally up to 2.5 m (8 feet) wide.

Range: Jeffrey pine occurs from the mountains in southwestern Oregon south through California to Baja California in Mexico. This includes the Klamath Mountains, coast ranges, Sierra Nevada, and mountains of Southern California.

Habitat: It grows in serpentine or non-serpentine soils, subalpine, mixed conifer, true fir, and yellow pine forests at low to high elevations from 60 to 3,100 m (200–10,200 feet). Sites at low elevations in the Klamath-Siskiyou Mountains are commonly serpentine, where it can grow with conifers and several evergreen hardwoods, or it may be the only conifer on some of those sites.

Associated Species: It is commonly associated with trees like Douglas fir, white fir, incense cedar, ponderosa pine, knobcone pine, lodgepole pine, Coulter pine, western white pine, red fir, giant sequoia (southern Sierra Nevada), western juniper, and hardwoods like black oak, canyon live oak, and interior live oak. It is uncommon in oak woodlands.

Similar Trees: Other similar three-needle pines include gray pine, Coulter pine, and ponderosa pine. Ponderosa pine has shorter asymmetrical cones with the scale prickles pointing outward. Jeffrey pine and ponderosa pine can hybridize, making identification difficult between the two. Bark between ponderosa pine and Jeffrey pine

Jeffrey pine
in stand of
other Jeffrey
pines

Bark

Bark

Cones

Needles

can be very similar, so cone differences are a better way to distinguish between the two species. Gray and Coulter pine have larger cones with long reflexed scales. Knobcone and Monterey have 3 shorter needles per bundle up to 15 cm (6 inches) in length.

Tree Risk Hazard Assessment

Biotic and Abiotic Factors: There are several factors that can cause mortality of Jeffrey pine, including insects and diseases such as armillaria root disease, black stain root disease, western dwarf mistletoe (*Arceuthobium campylopodum*), Jeffrey pine beetle, and pine engraver. Jeffrey pine is sensitive to air pollution, especially in Southern California. Other signs that indicate that a live tree may have failure potential include several heartwood conks on the main stem.

SUGAR PINE
Pinus lambertiana

Look For: For quick identification, look for a conical crown with long horizontal branches, very long cones (longest cones on the Pacific coast), reddish-brown bark with vertical furrowed plates, and a 5-needle bundle with twisted flexible needles.

Bark: The trunk is reddish brown and furrowed in rectangular vertical plates.

Needles: The needles are yellow green, 5 per bundle, 5–11 cm (2–4.5 inches) long, stiff, and usually twisted.

Cones: The cone is pendant, yellow brown, 20–60 cm (8–23 inches) long.

Height: It commonly grows to 40–60 m (130–195 feet) tall, occasionally up to 80 m (270 feet) tall. It has trunk diameters of 1.2–2.4 m (4–8 feet), occasionally up to 3.3 m (11 feet) wide.

Range: Sugar pine occurs from the mountains in central Oregon south through California to Baja California in Mexico. This includes the Cascades, coast ranges, Sierra Nevada, and mountains of Southern California.

Habitat: It grows in mixed conifer forests at middle elevations from 900 to 3,100 m (3,000–10,000 feet). It can occur in yellow pine, mixed evergreen, and true fir forests. It occurs on serpentine soils in areas of the Klamath-Siskiyou Mountains.

Associated Species: It is commonly associated with trees like Douglas fir, white fir, incense cedar, ponderosa pine, Jeffrey pine, red fir, giant sequoia (southern Sierra Nevada), and hardwoods like black oak, canyon live oak, and tan oak (Northern California and Oregon).

Similar Trees: Other similar 5-needle pines include western white pine and limber pine. Western white pine has a checkered-pattern bark with shorter cones and needles that are not twisted. Limber pine has much shorter mature cones, a different bark pattern, and needles somewhat stiff and curved. Whitebark, foxtail, and bristlecone pine are upper-subalpine species with much shorter cones.

Tree Risk Hazard Assessment

Biotic and Abiotic Factors: There are several factors that can cause mortality of sugar pine, including insects and diseases such as Heterobasidion root disease, dwarf mistletoe (*Arceuthobium californicum*), white pine blister rust, Ips beetle, and mountain bark beetle. Other signs that indicate a live tree may have failure potential include several heartwood conks on the main stem.

Sugar pine in mixed conifer forest

Bark

Cones

Needles

SINGLE-LEAF PINYON
Pinus monophylla

Look For: For quick identification, look for pinyon trees with a symmetrical or asymmetrical rounded crown, usually growing with junipers, short spheric cones, and 1 needle in a bundle.

Bark: The trunk is brownish, irregularly furrowed, and can be scaly.

Needles: The needles are usually 1 per bundle, 4–6 cm (1.5–2.5 inches) long, gray green to glaucous blue green. The needles are 3-sided.

Cones: The cone is spheric, light brown, and 6–9 cm (2.5–3.5 inches) long.

Height: It commonly grows 10–20 m (33–66 feet) tall. It has trunk diameters up to 80 cm (2.5 feet).

Range: Single-leaf pinyon occurs in southern Idaho, Utah, Nevada, Arizona, California, and Baja California in Mexico.

Habitat: It grows in pinyon/juniper woodland and yellow pine forests from 1,200 to 2,300 m (4,000–7,500 feet).

Associated Species: It is associated with trees like Sierra juniper, California juniper, Utah juniper, Jeffrey pine, and canyon live oak. Shrubs include big sagebrush, rabbitbrush, bitterbrush, and shrubby oaks.

Similar Trees: There are no other 1-needle pinyons on the Pacific coast. It can hybridize with Parry or 4-needle and 2-needle pinyon. Two-needle pinyon has 2 needles per bundle, and Parry pinyon has typically 4 needles per bundle. On the West Coast 2-needle pinyon occurs only in the Mohave Desert mountains of eastern to southeastern California. Parry pinyon occurs in pinyon juniper, chaparral, and yellow pine woods in south-central California and can vary from 2 to 5 needles per bundle. Lodgepole pine has similar cones, but has 2 needles per bundle and occurs higher in the mountains in Southern California, where their ranges may overlap.

Tree Risk Hazard Assessment

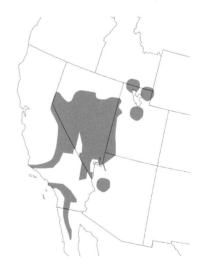

Biotic and Abiotic Factors: There are several factors that can cause mortality of single-leaf pinyon, including insects and diseases such as black stain root disease, pinyon dwarf mistletoe, and pinyon Ips beetle. Extensive heart rot may cause live tree failure.

Single-leaf pinyon in pinyon juniper woodland

Bark

Cones

Needles

WESTERN WHITE PINE
Pinus monticola

Look For: For quick identification, look for a conical symmetrical crown, long cones, gray to reddish-brown bark with square plates, and 5 needles in a bundle that are straight and flexible.

Bark: The trunk on mature trees is dark gray to orange brown, in square plates, and thin.

Needles: The needles are blue green, 5 per bundle, 5–11 cm (2–4.5 inches) long, somewhat flexible.

Cones: The cone is pendant, yellow brown, 12–32 cm (5–12 inches) long.

Height: It commonly grows 30–50 m (100–165 feet) tall, occasionally up to 70 m (230 feet) tall. It has trunk diameters from 1 m (3.2 feet), occasionally up to 2.4 m (8 feet) wide.

Range: Western white pine occurs from southern British Columbia south through Washington and Oregon, to the southern Sierra Nevada of California. From the Pacific Ocean, it occurs east through northern Idaho to northwestern Montana. This includes coast ranges, Klamath Mountains, Cascades, and northern Rocky Mountains. It is absent from foothill oak woodlands.

Habitat: It grows in a diversity of habitats including true fir, subalpine, lodgepole pine, Douglas fir–hemlock–cedar forests at low to high elevations of 0–3,400 m (0–11,150 feet). It occurs on serpentine soils in a variety of forest types at different elevations in the Klamath-Siskiyou Mountains.

Associated Species: It is commonly associated with trees like Pacific silver fir, grand fir, subalpine larch, western larch, Engelmann spruce, Douglas fir, white fir, lodgepole pine, whitebark pine, foxtail pine, limber pine, Jeffrey pine, red fir, mountain hemlock, and hardwoods like quaking aspen and paper birch. It additionally occurs with sugar pine, knobcone pine, and several evergreen hardwoods at low elevations on serpentine or non-serpentine soil in the Klamath-Siskiyou Mountains.

Similar Trees: Other similar 5-needle pines include sugar pine and limber pine. Sugar pine has more of a rectangular bark pattern with longer cones and needles that are twisted. Limber pine has shorter cones and a different bark pattern and needles somewhat curved. Whitebark, foxtail, and bristlecone pine are upper-subalpine species with much shorter cones.

Common bark color in Cascade Mountains

Western white pine in mesic mixed conifer forest

Common bark color in the high Sierra Nevada

Cones

Needles

Tree Risk Hazard Assessment

Biotic and Abiotic Factors: There are several factors that can cause mortality of western white pine, including insects and diseases such as armillaria root disease, dwarf mistletoe (*Arceuthobium monticola*), white pine blister rust, Ips beetle, and mountain bark beetle. Other signs that indicate that a live tree may have failure potential include several heartwood conks on the main stem.

BISHOP PINE
Pinus muricata

Look For: For quick identification, look for trees along the coast with a rounded asymmetrical crown, 2 medium-length needles per bundle, and cones with knobby tips that are whorled in around stems and branches.

Bark: The trunk is grayish brown with vertical plates and ridges.

Needles: The needles are green, 2 per bundle, 10–15 cm (3–6 inches) long.

Cones: The cone is asymmetric, light brown to brown, 5–10 cm (2–3 inches) long, and they tend to occur in whorls on branches and stems. The cone-scale tip knobs are thick, curved, and prickled.

Height: It commonly grows to 15–25 m (50–80 feet), occasionally up to 34 m (110 feet) tall. It has trunk diameters up to 90 cm (3 feet), occasionally 1.2 m (4 feet) wide.

Range: Bishop pine occurs along the coast from Curry County Oregon south to Santa Barbara County, California. It also occurs on a few islands off the California coast and in Baja California in Mexico.

Habitat: It grows in coastal forests (coastal chaparral on the Southern California coast) and redwood forests from 0 to 300 m (0–1,000 feet). It is less common in mixed evergreen forests.

Associated Species: It is commonly associated with trees like redwood, grand fir, Douglas fir, shore pine, Monterey pine, western hemlock, and several cypress species and hardwoods like tan oak, California bay, and Pacific madrone.

Similar Trees: Other similar pines include Monterey, shore, and knobcone pine. Knobcone pine has needles in threes and usually grows in areas away from the immediate coast. Shore pine has two shorter needles per bundle, and the trees are generally shorter. Monterey pine is widely planted along the Pacific coast and can occur with bishop pine or in close proximity to it. They appear very similar, but Monterey pine usually has needles in threes and the cones are slightly thicker.

Tree Risk Hazard Assessment

Biotic and Abiotic Factors: There are several factors that can cause mortality of bishop pine, including insects and diseases such as root rots, pitch canker, and the Ips beetle. Other signs that indicate a live tree may have failure potential include gall rusts on the stem.

Bishop pine in coastal forest

Bark

Needles

Cones

PONDEROSA PINE
Pinus ponderosa

Look For: For quick identification, look for a broad symmetrical crown, asymmetrical to symmetric cones with outward curving prickles on the scales, reddish-orange-brown bark in vertical plates, and 3 long needles in a bundle.

Bark: The trunk is reddish orange brown and has widely spaced shallow furrows in vertical rectangular plates.

Needles: The needles are yellow green, 3 per bundle, 7–26 cm (3–10 inches) long.

Cones: The cone is pendant, asymmetrical or symmetrical, yellow brown, 7–15 cm (3–6 inches) long. The prickles on the cone scales point straight or outward.

Height: It commonly grows 25–40 m (90–130 feet) tall, and variety *ponderosa* can grow up to 80 m (265 feet) tall. It has trunk diameters of 80–130 cm (2–4 feet), occasionally up to 3 m (9 feet) wide.

Range: Ponderosa pine occurs from British Columbia south through the western United States and into Mexico. From the Pacific Ocean, it occurs east to central Nebraska. There are two varieties in California and multiple varieties throughout its range. This book covers the varieties in the West Coast states from British Columbia to California, which include variety *ponderosa* (British Columbia to California; orange on the map) and *scopulorum* (eastern Oregon and Washington, but mainly Rocky Mountains; yellow on the map). Flora of North America describes what was previously called variety *washoensis* as its own species, Washoe pine (*Pinus washoensis*), which has a limited range in northeastern California at mid- to higher elevations.

Habitat: It occurs in yellow pine, mixed evergreen, and mixed conifer forests at low to middle elevations from 100 to 2,700 m (300–9,000 feet). Ponderosa pine is uncommon in subalpine forests. Additionally, Washoe pine can occur in lower subalpine forests and ultramafic soils from 1,400 to 3,000 m (5,000–9,800 feet) and have associates like western white pine and red fir.

Associated Species: It is commonly associated with trees like Douglas fir, big-cone Douglas fir, white fir, grand fir, incense cedar, sugar pine, Jeffrey pine, Coulter pine, gray pine, western juniper, lodgepole pine, giant sequoia (southern Sierra Nevada), and hardwoods like black oak, canyon live oak, interior live oak, and tan oak.

Similar Trees: Other similar long 3-needle pines include Jeffrey pine, Coulter pine, and

Ponderosa pine in mixed conifer forest

Bark

Cones

Needles

gray pine. Jeffrey pine has a longer and more symmetrical cone, with scale prickles pointing inward. Jeffrey pine usually grows at higher elevations than ponderosa pine and also on ultramafic soils (e.g., serpentine) at lower elevations adjacent to ponderosa pine stands. Jeffrey pine and ponderosa pine can hybridize, making identification difficult between the two. Coulter pine and gray pine have cones with large reflexed scale tips and usually do not have reddish-orange-brown bark. Gray pine usually has leaning stems compared to straight stems of ponderosa pine. Knobcone and Monterey pines have 3 shorter needles per bundle up to 15 cm (6 inches) in length. Washoe pine has cones similar to ponderosa pine but more symmetric and usually shorter, 7–10 cm (3–4 inches).

Washoe pine cones

Tree Risk Hazard Assessment

Biotic and Abiotic Factors: There are several factors that can cause mortality of ponderosa pine, including insects and diseases such Heterobasidion and black stain root disease, dwarf mistletoe, comandra blister rust, Ips beetle spp., western bark beetle, mountain bark beetle, and occasionally elytroderma needle cast and pine butterfly. Ponderosa pine is susceptible to air pollution, especially in Southern California. Other signs that indicate a tree or branches may have high failure potential include extensive cankers of western gall rust.

GRAY PINE
Pinus sabiniana

Look For: For quick identification, look for leaning trees in oak woodlands or chaparral areas with a rounded symmetrical or asymmetrical crown, 3 long needles per bundle, and large, heavy, dull-brown cones with reflexed scale tips that are continuous with the cone scale.

Bark: The bark is dark grayish brown, furrowed into irregular rectangular-shaped ridges that can appear orange-brown colored.

Needles: The needles are grayish green, 3 per bundle, 10–38 cm (4–15 inches) long.

Cones: The cone is pendant, ovate-oblong, dull brown, 15–30 cm (6–12 inches) long, and they tend to occur paired or can hang singly. The cone scales are elongated with reflexed tips and pointed.

Height: It commonly grows to 12–24 m (40–80 feet) tall, occasionally up to 32 m (105 feet) tall. It has trunk diameters of 30–90 cm (1–3 feet), occasionally up to 1.5 m (5 feet) wide. The trees are usually multistemmed and growing crooked or at an angle.

Range: Gray pine occurs in California from Siskiyou County to Ventura County. This includes Klamath, Cascade and Sierra Nevada foothills, and coast ranges.

Habitat: It grows in serpentine or non-serpentine soils in chaparral and oak woodlands from 300 to 2,100 m (980–6,900 feet). It is uncommon in mixed conifer forests.

Associated Species: It is commonly associated with trees like blue oak, interior live oak, canyon live oak, black oak, Oregon white oak, California buckeye, Macnab cypress, big-cone Douglas fir, Coulter pine, ponderosa pine, and western juniper. It can also grow in nearly pure stands with an understory of chaparral.

Similar Trees: Other similar 3-needle pines include Coulter pine. Coulter pine has longer cones that are yellow brown in color. Coulter pine trees are usually erect. Ponderosa and Jeffrey pine have cones without large reflexed scale tips. Knobcone and Monterey pine have shorter needles and cones that stay closed while on the tree.

Tree Risk Hazard Assessment

Biotic and Abiotic Factors: There are several factors that can cause mortality of gray pine, including insects and diseases such as Heterobasidion root disease, dwarf mistletoe (*Arceuthobium occidentale*), and Ips spp. beetle.

Gray pine in oak woodland

Bark

Cones

Needles

WESTERN SYCAMORE
Platanus racemosa

Look For: For quick identification, look for a tree with a rounded or spreading asymmetrical crown, patchwork of different colors beneath the peeled bark, large lobed alternate leaves, growing near riparian areas, and leafless in the winter months.

Bark: The trunk is a patchwork of white, tawny beige, pinkish gray, and pale brown, with older bark becoming darker and peeling away.

Leaves: The leaves are alternate, green, palmately lobed, 10–25 cm (4–10 inches) long and wide, and glabrous to hairy.

Fruit: The fruit is spherical, 2–3 cm (0.8–1.2 inches) in diameter, and appears bristly from the numerous projecting achenes.

Height: It commonly grows to 10–35 m (35–115 feet) tall. It has trunk diameters of less than 1 m (3 feet), occasionally up to 2 m (6.5 feet) wide.

Range: Western sycamore occurs from north-central California through the western half of Southern California into Baja California in Mexico. This includes the Sacramento and San Joaquin Valleys, central and southern coast ranges, and in the Southern California mountains and valleys.

Habitat: It grows in riparian areas from 0 to 2,400 m (0–7,800 feet).

Associated Species: It is commonly associated with trees like white alder, California walnut, coast live oak, valley oak, willows, and California bay.

Similar Trees: Other trees with similar leaf shape are big-leaf maple and black oak. Big-leaf maple has opposite leaves and a different bark pattern. Black oak leaves have a more elliptic leaf shape than the overall circular shape of sycamore and leaf lobes that are sharper pointed, and black oak occurs in upland habitats.

Tree Risk Hazard Assessment

Biotic and Abiotic Factors: There are several factors that can cause mortality of western sycamore, including insects and diseases such as armillaria root disease, Phytophthora root rot, and invasive shot-hole borer. Other signs that indicate a live tree may have failure potential include extensive stem decay. It is unusual to find large standing dead sycamore more than one year after mortality, especially since many trees are naturally leaning while alive.

Western sycamore in riparian area

Stem pattern without outer bark

Fruit

Leaf

PLAINS COTTONWOOD
Populus deltoides ssp. *monilifera*

Look For: For quick identification, look for a tree with a broadly rounded crown and a single stem, heart-shaped leaves with crenate leaf edges, whitish to grayish furrowed bark, growing near streams or floodplains, and leafless in the winter months.

Bark: The trunk is whitish and smooth on young trees, becoming grayish, thick, and deeply furrowed with wide flat ridges with age.

Leaves: The leaves are alternate, deltoid or heart-shaped with an abrupt, elongate tip, coarsely toothed or crenate, 5–12 cm (2–5 inches) long and wide, green, glabrous. The winter buds are long pointed, dark yellow with yellowish resin.

Fruit: The flowers are elongate catkins and the fruit is a capsule, ovoid to pear-shaped.

Height: It commonly grows to 8–30 m (25–100 feet) and up to 35 m (110 feet) tall. It has trunk diameters of 0.3–1 m (1–3 feet) up to 2 m (6.5 feet) wide.

Range: Eastern cottonwood (*Populus deltoides*) occurs in southern Canada, the Rocky Mountains, and all of the eastern United States. There are three subspecies: *monilifera*, *deltoides*, *wislizeni*. Plains cottonwood (*Populus deltoides monilifera*) occurs in eastern Washington, eastern Oregon, and southeastern British Columbia. These are native trees or possibly introduced from populations in the eastern Rockies.

Habitat: It grows along streams in riparian areas along the Snake River and Columbia River drainages in eastern Washington, eastern Oregon, and southeastern British Columbia.

Associated Species: It is commonly associated with trees like black cottonwood, box elder, Russian olive, silver maple, and willows.

Similar Trees: Other trees with similar leaf shape are black cottonwood, Fremont cottonwood, and quaking aspen. Black cottonwood has ovate leaves that are gradually narrowed to a slender tip and has spherical or round capsules. Quaking aspen has non-resinous buds and leaves that are more circular than plains cottonwood and often occurs in habitats at higher elevations. Fremont cottonwood has spherical or round capsules, with which it can overlap in range in the southern Rocky Mountains but does not overlap ranges on the Pacific coast.

Plains cottonwood in riparian area

Leaves and fruit

Leaves and fruit

Tree Risk Hazard Assessment

Biotic and Abiotic Factors: There are several factors that can cause mortality of plains cottonwood including insects and diseases such as armillaria root disease, Cytospora cankers, and several insect borers. Other signs that indicate a live tree may have high failure potential include several conks on the main stem. Trees are susceptible to fires.

Bark

FREMONT COTTONWOOD
Populus fremontii

Look For: For quick identification, look for a tree with a broadly rounded crown and a single stem, heart-shaped leaves with crenate margins, whitish or grayish furrowed bark, growing near streams or floodplains, and leafless in the winter months.

Bark: The trunk is whitish and smooth on young trees, becoming grayish, furrowed, and fissured with age.

Leaves: The leaves are alternate, deltate or heart-shaped, with an abrupt, elongate tip, 5–10 cm (2–4 inches) long and wide, green, glabrous. The winter buds are long pointed, yellow brown with yellowish resin.

Fruit: The flowers are elongate catkins, and the fruit is a small round capsule.

Height: It commonly grows 12–35 m (40–115 feet) tall. It has trunk diameters of 0.6–1 m (2–3 feet), up to 1.5 m (4.5 feet) wide.

Range: Fremont cottonwood occurs in the western United States in Nevada, Utah, Colorado, Arizona, New Mexico, and California and northern Mexico. This includes most of California.

Habitat: It grows along streams and floodplains in riparian forests from 0 to 2,400 m (0–7,800 feet).

Associated Species: It is commonly associated with trees like box elder, big-leaf maple, ash spp., red alder, sycamore, coast live oak, California walnut, salt cedar, and willows.

Similar Trees: Other trees with similar leaf shape are black cottonwood, quaking aspen, and plains cottonwood. Black cottonwood has ovate leaves that are gradually narrowed to a slender tip and usually occurs at higher elevations where they occur together. Quaking aspen has leaves that are more circular than Fremont cottonwood and occurs more in habitats at higher elevations. Plains cottonwood has a pear-shaped capsule and occurs to the north of Fremont cottonwood on the Pacific coast.

Tree Risk Hazard Assessment

Biotic and Abiotic Factors: There are several factors that can cause mortality of Fremont cottonwood, including insects and diseases such as armillaria root disease, cankers, and insect borers. Other signs that indicate a live tree may have

Fremont cottonwood in riparian area

Bark

Leaves and fruit

Leaves

high failure potential include multiple cankers on the main stem. Since cotton-woods can occur along streamsides, roots loosened by water can increase failure potential.

QUAKING ASPEN
Populus tremuloides

Look For: For quick identification, look for a tree with a rounded crown and a single stem, heart-shaped to nearly round leaves with a short abrupt tip, greenish-white to light-gray bark with blackish markings, yellow-leaved trees in the fall, and leafless in the winter months.

Bark: The trunk is greenish white to whitish, smooth, and marked with horizontal streaks and black knots.

Leaves: The leaves are alternate, crenate edged, heart-shaped to nearly round with a rounded base and abruptly short pointed to an acute tip, 4–8 cm (1.5–3.5 inches) long, green on top, glaucous on bottom.

Fruit: The flowers are elongate catkins, and the fruit is a small capsule that resembles a patch of cotton when it opens.

Height: It commonly grows 15–20 m (50–65 feet) tall and occasionally up to 27 m (90 feet). It has trunk diameters of 20–80 cm (0.65–2.6 feet) and up to 120 cm (4 feet) wide.

Range: Quaking aspen occurs from Alaska south through British Columbia, Washington, Oregon, and California to northern Mexico to Baja California, Mexico. From the Pacific Ocean, it occurs east across Canada, the northern half of the United States, and the Rocky Mountain states. On the Pacific coast, this includes coast ranges, Klamath Mountains, Cascades, Sierra Nevada, and Southern California mountains.

Habitat: It grows in true fir, lodgepole pine, yellow pine, mixed conifer forests from 460 to 3,150 m (1,500–10,300 feet). It also occurs in riparian areas. It can occur in monoculture or pure stands on the Pacific coast; however, that is much more common in the Rockies (i.e., Utah and Colorado).

Associated Species: It is commonly associated with trees like white spruce (British Columbia and Alaska), Engelmann spruce, ponderosa pine, Douglas fir, white fir, red fir, western juniper, grand juniper, Jeffrey pine, lodgepole pine, black cottonwood, balsam poplar, and paper birch.

Similar Trees: Other trees with similar leaf shape are Fremont cottonwood, plains cottonwood, and black cottonwood. Fremont and plains cottonwood have deltate or heart-shaped leaves that

Quaking aspens of different heights

Bark

Leaves and fruit

Leaves

are cordate or truncate at the base and usually occurs at lower elevations where they grow together geographically with quaking aspen. Black cottonwood has leaves that are more ovate with a long tapered tip and gray furrowed bark. Alders are serrated on the leaf edges.

Tree Risk Hazard Assessment

Biotic and Abiotic Factors: There are a numerous biotic and abiotic problems that could cause mortality of quaking aspen. Several insects and diseases can contribute to quaking aspen mortality including Hypoxylon cankers, Ceratocystis black canker, sooty bark canker, cryptosphaeria canker, aspen leaf miner, and forest tent caterpillar. Other signs that indicate a live tree may have high failure potential include one or more conks on the main stem (especially Ganoderma or Phellinus trunk rot), crytosphaeria canker, ceratocystis black canker, and poplar borer damage. Quaking aspen is very susceptible to fire.

BLACK COTTONWOOD
Populus trichocarpa

Look For: For quick identification, look for a tree with a broadly rounded or conical crown and a single stem, ovate-shaped leaves with long tapered tip, 3- or 4-valved capsule, gray furrowed bark, growing near streams, and leafless in the winter months.

Bark: The trunk is grayish white, smooth and with lenticels on young trees, becoming gray and fissured with age.

Leaves: The leaves are alternate, crenate edged, narrowly to widely ovate with a rounded base and tapered to an acute tip, elongate tip, 7–20 cm (2.75–8 inches) long, green on top, glaucous on bottom. The winter buds are reddish, red resinous, and fragrant, which aids in identification.

Fruit: The flowers are elongate catkins, and the fruit is a small capsule.

Height: It commonly grows 30–50 m (98–164 feet) tall. It has trunk diameters of 1–1.5 m (3.5–5 feet) and up to 2 m (6.6 feet) wide.

Range: Black cottonwood occurs from south-central Alaska to British Columbia, south through Washington and Oregon, south through California to Baja California, Mexico. From the Pacific Ocean, it occurs east to western Alberta, North Dakota, Wyoming, and Utah. Some authors recognize black cottonwood as a subspecies of balsam poplar (*Populus balsamifera*).

Habitat: It grows in Douglas fir–hemlock–cedar, subboreal white spruce hardwood, and riparian forests from 0 to 2,800 m (0–9,200 feet).

Associated Species: It is commonly associated with trees like western hemlock, western red cedar, Sitka spruce, white spruce, grand fir, Douglas fir, white fir, western juniper, Jeffrey pine, lodgepole pine, and hardwoods like box elder, big-leaf maple, white alder, red alder, Oregon white ash, sycamore, California laurel, coast live oak, quaking aspen, and willows.

Similar Trees: Other trees with similar leaf shape are Fremont and plains cottonwood, quaking aspen, and balsam polar. Fremont and plains cottonwood have deltate leaves that are cordate or truncate at the base. Fremont cottonwood usually occurs at lower elevations, where it grows together with black cottonwood geographically. Quaking aspen has leaves that are more circular than black cottonwood and has a more whitish bark on mature trees. Balsam polar is very similar and has 2 (3) valved capsules. Balsam poplar and

Black cottonwood with conifers in the background

Bark

Leaves and fruit

black cottonwood also hybridize where they occur together in the subboreal white spruce hardwoods zone in southern Alaska and northern British Columbia, making identification more difficult.

Tree Risk Hazard Assessment

Biotic and Abiotic Factors: There are a few factors that can cause mortality of black cottonwood, including diseases such as Cytospora cankers. Other signs that indicate a live tree may have failure include several heartwood conks on the main stem. Since cottonwoods can occur along streamsides, roots loosened by water can increase failure potential.

Leaves

BIG-CONE DOUGLAS FIR
Pseudotsuga macrocarpa

Look For: For quick identification, look for trees with a conical crown on steep protected slopes in chaparral or bordering forested areas or mixed forest, cones with exserted bracts, and growing in Southern California.

Bark: The trunk is grayish brown with deep vertical ridges.

Needles: The needles are green, pointed, flexible, 2.5–4.5 cm (1–1.8 inches) long, and spiraled around the stem.

Cones: The cones are pendant, 11–17 cm (4.5–6.5 inches) with exserted tridentine bracts.

Height: It commonly grows 15–30 m (50–100 feet) tall, occasionally up to 40 m (130 feet) tall. It has trunk diameters of 50–150 cm (1.6–5 feet), occasionally up to 2 m (6.5 feet) wide.

Range: Big-cone Douglas fir occurs in Southern California from Santa Barbara and Kern Counties south to San Diego County.

Habitat: It grows in protected areas in chaparral, mixed evergreen, and up to mixed conifer forests from 200 to 2,400 m (650–7,800 feet).

Associated Species: It is commonly associated with trees like Coulter pine, ponderosa pine, knobcone pine, Jeffrey pine, incense cedar, sugar pine, white fir, and hardwoods like California bay, coast live oak, black oak, canyon live oak, and interior live oak.

Similar Trees: Other similar trees include Douglas fir and white fir. Big-cone Douglas fir has larger and longer cones than Douglas fir, and their native ranges do not overlap. White fir has upright cones and blunt needles that are green to whitish green.

Tree Risk Hazard Assessment

Biotic and Abiotic Factors: There are a few factors that can cause mortality of big-cone Douglas fir, one being armillaria root disease. It is very normal to see dead big-cone Douglas firs still standing more than a few years after mortality. Other signs that indicate that a live tree may have failure potential include several heartwood conks on the main stem.

Big-cone Douglas fir in mixed evergreen forest

Bark

Cones

Needles

DOUGLAS FIR
Pseudotsuga menziesii

Look For: For quick identification, look for trees with a conical crown with gray to brown furrowed and ridged bark, flexible needles spiraling around the stem and scented, and cones with exserted bracts.

Bark: The trunk is grayish to red brown with fissures, deep vertical ridges, and has thick bark with age.

Needles: The green leaves pointed, flexible, 2–4 cm (0.75–1.5 inches) long, and spiraled around the stem. The branches have pointed buds.

Cones: The cone is pendant, brown, 4–10 cm (1.5–4 inches), with exserted tridentine bracts.

Height: Variety *menziesii* along the Pacific coast can commonly grow 20–75 m (75–250 feet) tall, occasionally up to 100 m (330 feet) tall. It has trunk diameters of 150–180 cm (5–6 feet), occasionally up to 4 m (13 feet) wide. Variety *glauca* is smaller and can reach 50 m (160 feet tall) and diameters up to 1.5 m (5 feet).

Range: Douglas fir (variety *menziesii*) occurs from western British Columbia south through Washington and Oregon to central California (shaded blue on map). This includes the Cascades, coast ranges, and northern Sierra Nevada. Variety glauca occurs from north-central British Columbia south through the Rocky Mountains to central Mexico (shaded orange on map).

Habitat: It occurs in Douglas fir, Douglas fir–hemlock–cedar, Douglas fir–grand fir, true fir, mixed conifer and mixed evergreen, and Oregon white oak woodland from 0 to 2,200 m (0–7,500 feet). It is uncommon to absent in upper subalpine forests.

Associated Species: It is commonly associated with trees like western hemlock, Pacific silver fir, noble fir, redwood, white fir, sugar pine, incense cedar, ponderosa pine, lodgepole pine, Port Orford cedar (northwestern California), and hardwoods like Pacific madrone, tan oak, giant chinquapin, red alder, coast live oak, black oak, canyon live oak, Oregon white oak, and additionally white spruce, paper birch, and quaking aspen in British Columbia.

Similar Trees: Other trees with similar needles include big-cone Douglas fir, hemlocks, spruces, and true firs. Big-cone Douglas fir has larger and longer cones than Douglas fir, and their native ranges do not overlap. Hemlocks

Douglas fir in Douglas fir–hemlock–cedar forest

Bark

Cones

Needles

have shorter needles and cones without exserted bracts. Spruces have stiff pointed to sharp needles and cones without exserted bracts. True firs have upright cones and needles that are either flattened or curving upward. Hemlock needles are shorter and the cones lack the exserted bracts. Douglas fir needles have a distinct scent that differs from other conifers.

Tree Risk Hazard Assessment

Biotic and Abiotic Factors: There are several factors that can cause mortality of Douglas fir, including insects and diseases such as armillaria root disease, laminated root rot, black stain root disease, dwarf mistletoe, Swiss needle cast, western spruce budworm, Douglas fir tussock moth, Douglas fir beetle, and flat-headed fir borer. Other signs that indicate a live tree may have high failure potential include one or more conks on the main stem (brown trunk rot, schweinitzii butt rot).

COAST LIVE OAK
Quercus agrifolia

Look For: For quick identification, look for a tree with a spreading crown, alternate, spiny margined, strongly convex, evergreen leaves and somewhat smooth bark, and acorns.

Bark: The trunk is gray to dark gray and slightly furrowed and platy. Chunks of bark fall off with age.

Leaves: The leaves are shiny dark green on top and convex, dull blue green, and glabrous to hairy (variety *oxydenia*) beneath, evergreen, oblong to ovate, 2.5–8 cm (1–3 inches) long, and spiny toothed.

Fruit: The acorn cup is 10–18 mm (0.4–0.7 inch) wide, while the nut is 25–35 mm (1–1.4 inches) long.

Height: It commonly grows 10–25 m (35–85 feet) tall. It has trunk diameters of 30–120 cm (1–4 feet).

Range: Coast live oak occurs from the coast of Northern California south through California to northern Mexico. This includes the north and south California coast ranges and mountains of Southern California.

Habitat: It grows in canyons, slopes, and ridges in mixed evergreen, oak woodlands, and riparian areas from 0 to 1,200 m (0–4,000 feet).

Associated Species: It is commonly associated with hardwoods like black oak, Engelmann oak, blue oak, big-leaf maple, California bay, Pacific madrone, California walnut, and western sycamore.

Similar Trees: Other similar evergreen oaks include interior live oak, Shreve oak, canyon live oak, and Engelmann oak. Interior live oak has shiny lower leaf surfaces, but the leaves are flat, not convex. Canyon live oak has golden hairy or dull whitish lower leaf surfaces and flat leaves. Shreve oak has leaves that are flat to slightly convex with olive-green lower surfaces. Engelmann oak leaves are blue green and not spiny margined. Some smaller shrubby oaks can appear similar to young coast live oak. Coast live oak can hybridize with black oak, interior live oak, and Shreve oak.

Tree Risk Hazard Assessment

Biotic and Abiotic Factors: There are several factors that can cause mortality of coast live oak, including insects and diseases such as armillaria root disease, sudden oak death disease, and oak ambrosia beetle (*Monarthrum*). Other signs that indicate a live tree may have high failure

Coast live oak in open oak woodland

potential include one or more conks on the main stem (white trunk rot), oak ambrosia beetle signs, or with cankers (one-third of the stem with sudden oak death disease).

Bark

Fruit

Leaf

Variety *oxydenia* showing hairy leaf underside

CANYON LIVE OAK
Quercus chrysolepis

Look For: For quick identification, look for a tree with a spreading crown, alternate, flattened evergreen leaves that are golden hairy or whitish beneath, leaves are toothed or entire, and has acorns.

Bark: The trunk is light gray and has irregular rectangular scaly plates.

Leaves: The leaves are shiny dark green on top, dull golden hairy beneath (turning whitish with age), evergreen, elliptic to ovate, 2.5–8 cm (1–3.2 inches) long, alternate, and toothed or entire.

Fruit: The acorn cup is 16–30 mm (0.6–1.2 inches) wide, while the nut is 25–30 mm (1–1.2 inches) long.

Height: It commonly grows 6–30 m (20–100 feet) tall. It has trunk diameters of 30–100 cm (1–3.2 feet). The shrub form of canyon live oak with smaller leaves has been called variety *nana*; however, in this book, they are all placed in *Quercus chrysolepis*.

Range: Canyon live oak occurs from the mountains and valleys in central Oregon south through California to northern Mexico, and east to Arizona and southwestern New Mexico. This includes the Cascades, coast ranges, Sierra Nevada, and mountains of Southern California.

Habitat: It grows in chaparral, mixed evergreen, and yellow pine forests from 100 to 2,700 m (330–8,800 feet). It is uncommon in low-elevation foothill oak woodlands.

Associated Species: It is commonly associated with trees like Douglas fir, bigcone Douglas fir, white fir, incense cedar, Coulter pine, ponderosa pine, sugar pine, single-needle pinyon, and hardwoods like Oregon white oak, big-leaf maple, California bay, Pacific madrone, tan oak, and interior live oak. In chaparral it occurs with Ceanothus and shrubby oaks.

Similar Trees: Other similar evergreen oaks include interior live oak, coast live oak, tan oak, giant chinquapin. Interior live oak has shiny lower leaf surfaces. Coast live oak has convex leaves that are always spine toothed on the leaf margins. Tan oak has convex leaf margins and indented veins on the tops of the leaves. Giant chinquapin can have very similar leaves, but they tend to be longer, smooth margined, and a more permanent golden color on the undersides. Numerous smaller shrubby oaks can appear similar to young

Canyon live oak in mixed evergreen forest

Bark

Fruit

Leaves

canyon live oak. Canyon live oak can hybridize with island oak and smaller shrubby oaks.

Tree Risk Hazard Assessment

Biotic and Abiotic Factors: There are several factors that can cause mortality of canyon live oak, including insects and diseases such as armillaria root disease, crown rot (Phytophthora), sudden oak death disease, golden-spotted oak borer, and invasive shot-hole borer. Other signs that indicate a live tree may have high failure potential include a decayed stem or a stem with cankers (one-third of the stem with sudden oak death disease).

BLUE OAK
Quercus douglasii

Look For: For quick identification, look for a tree with a rounded to spreading crown that has blue-green, alternate leaves with shallow rounded lobes or entire, persistent, or deciduous leaves in the winter months, and acorns.

Bark: The trunk is gray, somewhat scaly, and checkered into rectangular plates.

Leaves: The pale blue-green leaves are semi-deciduous, 4–10 cm (1.5–4 inches) long, alternate, irregularly shallow lobed or entire, with rounded tips. Some trees have persistent leaves, while others lose them in the winter months.

Fruit: The acorn cup is 10–20 mm (0.4–0.8 inch) wide, while the nut is 20–35 mm (0.8–1.4 inches) long with a pointed tip.

Height: It commonly grows 6–20 m (20–66 feet) tall, occasionally up to 35 m (120 feet) tall. It has trunk diameters of 35–60 cm (1–2 feet), occasionally up to 2 m (6.5 feet) wide.

Range: Blue oak occurs in California from Shasta County to Los Angeles County. This includes the Cascade–Sierra Nevada foothills, Sacramento–San Joaquin Valleys, and coast ranges

Habitat: It grows in oak woodlands and annual grasslands from 30 to 1,900 m (100–6,200 feet).

Associated Species: It is commonly associated with trees like gray pine, interior live oak, California buckeye, coast live oak, valley oak, Oregon white oak, canyon live oak, and California juniper.

Similar Trees: Other similar oaks with lobed leaves include black oak, Oregon white oak, and valley oak. Black oak has larger leaves and deeper lobes with pointed tips. Oregon white oak and valley oak have rounded leaf lobes that are more deeply lobed than blue oak. Blue oak can hybridize with the Oregon white oak and valley oak.

Tree Risk Hazard Assessment

Biotic and Abiotic Factors: There are a few factors that can cause mortality of blue oak, including diseases such as armillaria root disease and canker or heart rot (*Inonotus dryophilus*). Other signs that indicate that a live tree may have failure potential include one or more conks or cankers on the main stem from heart rot.

Blue oak in oak woodland

Fruit and leaves

Bark

Leaves

ENGELMANN OAK
Quercus engelmannii

Look For: For quick identification, look for a tree with a spreading crown, blue-green alternate, oblong, entire leaves, persistent or deciduous leaves in the winter months, and acorns.

Bark: The trunk is gray, checkered into thick scales.

Leaves: The pale blue-green leaves are semi-deciduous, 4–19 cm (1.5–3.5 inches) long, alternate, oblong, entire, occasionally toothed or slightly lobed, with rounded tips. Some trees have persistent leaves, while others lose them in the winter months.

Fruit: The acorn cup is 12–18 mm (0.5–0.7 inch) wide, while the nut is 15–25 mm (0.6–1 inch) long with a mostly rounded tip.

Height: It commonly grows 5–15 m (15–50 feet) tall, occasionally up to 20 m (65 feet) tall. It has trunk diameters of 36–60 cm (1–2 feet) and up to 1 m (40 inches).

Range: Engelmann oak has limited distribution and occurs in southwestern California and slightly into northwestern Mexico. In California it occurs mainly in Los Angeles, Riverside, Orange, and San Diego Counties.

Habitat: It grows in oak woodlands from 150 to 1,250 m (500–4,000 feet).

Associated Species: It is commonly associated with coast live oak and also black oak, walnut, California sycamore, and cottonwood.

Similar Trees: Other similar oaks include blue oak. Blue oak has similar-colored leaves that are either entire or mostly shallowly lobed. The ranges of Engelmann and blue oak slightly overlap. Coast live oak has shinier green leaves with toothed margins. It can hybridize with valley oak.

Tree Risk Hazard Assessment

Biotic and Abiotic Factors: There are a few factors that can cause mortality of Engelmann oak, including insects and diseases such as root rot and invasive shot-hole borer. Other signs that indicate a live tree may have failure potential include one or more conks on the main stem from brown rot.

Engelmann oak in oak woodland

Bark

Fruit and leaves

OREGON WHITE OAK
Quercus garryana var. *garryana*

Look For: For quick identification, look for a tree with a rounded to spreading crown, dark-green alternate leaves with deep rounded lobes, gray checkered bark, deciduous leaves in the winter months, and round-tipped acorns.

Bark: The trunk is gray, checkered with age.

Leaves: The dark-green leaves are deciduous, 5–15 cm (2–6 inches) long, alternate, irregularly lobed, with rounded tips.

Fruit: The acorn cup is 10–25 mm (0.4–1 inch) wide, while the nut is 20–30 mm (0.8–1.2 inches) long with a rounded tip.

Height: It commonly grows 8–30 m (30–100 feet) tall, occasionally up to 35 m (120 feet) tall. It has trunk diameters of 60–100 cm (2–3.5 feet), occasionally up to 2.4 m (8 feet) wide. The shrub varieties *semota* and *breweri* grow less than 5 m (15 feet) tall.

Range: Oregon white oak occurs from southwestern British Columbia through western Washington and western Oregon to much of Northern California and part of the Sierra Nevada.

Habitat: It grows in oak woodland, yellow pine, and mixed evergreen forest from 0 to 2,200 m (0–7,300 feet). The shrub varieties can occur in mixed conifer forests.

Associated Species: It is commonly associated with trees like black oak, big-leaf maple, canyon live oak, Pacific madrone, California bay, Oregon ash, and conifers like Douglas fir, grand fir, gray pine, western juniper, and ponderosa pine.

Similar Trees: Other similar oaks with lobed leaves include black oak, valley, and blue oak. Black oak has leaves with pointed lobes. Valley oak is very similar and has pointed acorns tips. Oregon white oak can be challenging to distinguish from valley oak. Blue oak has smaller leaves that are blue green and shallowly lobed to entire. Oregon white oak can hybridize with blue oak and valley oak.

Tree Risk Hazard Assessment

Biotic and Abiotic Factors: There are a few factors that can cause mortality of Oregon white oak, including diseases such as armillaria root disease and white pocket rot (Inonotus dryophilus). Other signs that indicate a live tree may have high failure potential include one or more conks on the main stem of white pocket rot.

Oregon white oak in oak woodland

Bark

Fruit and leaves

Leaf

BLACK OAK
Quercus kelloggii

Look For: For quick identification, look for a tree with a broadly rounded to spreading crown that has alternate lobed leaves with acute pointed lobes, oblong in overall leaf shape, fallen leaves in the winter months, and acorns.

Bark: The trunk is dark gray brown, checkered and deeply furrowed with age.

Leaves: The green leaves are deciduous, 9–20 cm (3.5–8 inches) long, alternate, irregularly lobed with bristle tips.

Fruit: The acorn cup is 16–25 mm (0.6–1 inch) wide, while the nut is 20–35 mm (0.8–1.4) long.

Height: It commonly grows to 10–25 m (30–80 feet) tall, occasionally up to 35 m (120 feet) tall. It has trunk diameters of 0.3–1.5 m (1–5 feet), occasionally up to 1.8 m (6 feet) wide.

Range: Black oak occurs from the mountains and valleys in south-central Oregon south through California to Baja California in Mexico. This includes the Cascades, coast ranges, Sierra Nevada, and mountains of Southern California.

Habitat: It grows in yellow pine forest, oak woodlands, mixed evergreen, and mixed conifer forests from 30 to 2,600 m (100–8,500 feet).

Associated Species: It is commonly associated with trees like Douglas fir, white fir, incense cedar, knobcone pine, ponderosa pine, giant sequoia (southern Sierra Nevada), and hardwoods like Oregon white oak, coast live oak, canyon live oak, valley oak, California bay, and Pacific madrone.

Similar Trees: Other similar oaks with lobed leaves include Oregon white oak and valley oak. Oregon white oak and valley oak have rounded leaf lobes. Bigleaf maple can look similar but has opposite leaves. California sycamore has lobed leaves, but the trunk is white and mottled. Black oak can hybridize with interior live oak and coast live oak.

Tree Risk Hazard Assessment

Biotic and Abiotic Factors: There are several factors that can cause mortality of black oak, including insects and diseases such as armillaria root disease, Canker or heart rot (*Inonotus dryophilus*), sudden oak death disease, and golden-spotted oak borer. Other signs that indicate a live tree may have high failure potential include a decayed stem or a stem with cankers (one-third of the stem with sudden oak death disease).

Black oak in mixed evergreen forest

Fruit

Bark

Oak mistletoe on black oak tree in early spring

Leaves

VALLEY OAK
Quercus lobata

Look For: For quick identification, look for a tree with a spreading crown that has dark-green alternate leaves with deep rounded lobes, deciduous leaves in the winter months, common in riparian areas, and acorns with pointed tips.

Bark: The trunk is gray, checkered with age.

Leaves: The dark-green leaves are deciduous, 5–12 cm (2–4.8 inches) long, alternate, irregularly lobed, with rounded tips.

Fruit: The acorn cup is 14–30 mm (0.55–1.2 inches) wide, while the nut is 30–50 mm (1.2–2 inches) long with a pointed tip.

Height: It commonly grows 10–25 m (30–75 feet) tall, occasionally up to 40 m (130 feet) tall. It has trunk diameters of 50–70 cm (1.8–2.4 feet), occasionally up to 2.4 m (8 feet) wide.

Range: Valley oak occurs in California from Shasta County to Los Angeles County. This includes the Cascade–Sierra Nevada foothills, Sacramento–San Joaquin Valleys, and coast ranges.

Habitat: It grows in oak woodland and riparian forests from 0 to 775 m (0–2,500 feet).

Associated Species: It is commonly associated with trees like box-elder, maple, Oregon ash, white alder, black walnut, western sycamore, Fremont cottonwood, interior live oak, coast live oak, valley oak, black oak, and black willow.

Similar Trees: Other similar oaks with lobed leaves include black oak, Oregon white oak, and blue oak. Black oak has leaves with pointed lobes. Oregon white oak has rounded acorn tips that are shorter in length. Oregon white oak can be challenging to distinguish from valley oak. Blue oak has smaller leaves that are blue green and shallowly lobed to entire. Valley oak can hybridize with Oregon white oak, blue oak, and Engelmann oak.

Tree Risk Hazard Assessment

Biotic and Abiotic Factors: There are several factors that can cause mortality of valley oak, including insects and diseases such as armillaria root disease, Canker or heart rot (*Inonotus dryophilus*), invasive shot-hole borer, and Mediterranean oak borer. Other signs that indicate a live tree may have high failure potential include one or more conks or cankers on the main stem from heart rot and oak ambrosia beetle signs.

Valley oak in oak woodland

Bark

Fruit

Leaves

INTERIOR LIVE OAK
Quercus wislizeni

Look For: For quick identification, look for a tree with a spreading or somewhat narrow crown that has alternate, flat, evergreen leaves around 5 cm (2 inches) long that are shiny green on both surfaces, leaves are toothed or entire, and acorns.

Bark: The trunk is grayish and smooth, becoming cracked with rectangular scaly plates with age.

Leaves: The green leaves are shiny dark green on top, lighter shiny yellow-green beneath, evergreen, elliptic to ovate, 2–5 cm (1–2 inches) long, alternate, toothed or entire.

Fruit: The acorn cup is 14–30 mm (0.55–1.2 inches) wide, while the nut is 30–50 mm (1.2–2 inches) long with a pointed tip. The acorn cup is 12–18 mm (0.5–0.7 inch) wide, while the acorn is 20–40 mm (0.75–1.5 inches) long.

Height: It commonly grows 10–23 m (33–75 feet) tall. There are usually one to several trunks up to 0.5 m (1 foot) wide. The shorter form of interior live oak in California with smaller leaves is usually tall-shrub size, 2–6 m (7–20 feet), and has been treated as variety *frutescens*.

Range: Interior live oak occurs throughout much of the lower elevations in California south to northern Mexico. This includes the Cascades, coast ranges, and the Sierra Nevada. It grows at mid-elevations in the mountains of Southern California. Shreve oak is included in the range distribution map.

Habitat: It grows in canyons, valleys, and foothills in chaparral, riparian, mixed evergreen, and oak woodlands from 300 to 1,900 m (1,000–6,200 feet).

Associated Species: It is commonly associated with trees like big-cone Douglas fir, Coulter pine, gray pine, knobcone pine, and hardwoods like Oregon white oak, valley oak, blue oak, coast live oak, Oregon white oak, and Engelmann oak. In chaparral it occurs with chamise, manzanita, Ceanothus, and Quercus shrubs.

Similar Trees: Other similar evergreen oaks include Shreve oak, coast live oak, and canyon live oak. *Quercus parvula* var. *shrevei* (Shreve oak), still considered part of *Quercus wislizeni* on efloras.org. Shreve oak occurs along the California coast, usually in the form of a single-stemmed tree, and has leaves that are nearly identical but longer (up to 9 cm/3.5 inches long) and leaf undersides being duller olive green. Shreve oak

Interior live oak in oak woodland

Bark of interior live oak

Fruit

Leaves

bark appears to be more furrowed and ridged than interior live oak. Canyon live oak has golden hairy to whitish dull lower leaf surfaces. Coast live oak has convex leaves. Several smaller shrubby oaks can appear similar to young interior live oak. Interior live oak can hybridize with coast live oak and black oak.

Leaves of Shreve oak

Tree Risk Hazard Assessment

Biotic and Abiotic Factors: There are a few factors that can cause mortality of interior live oak, including diseases such as armillaria root disease and crown rot. Interior live oak is not very susceptible to sudden oak death. However, Shreve oak is susceptible. Other signs that indicate a live tree may have high failure potential include one or more conks on the main stem (white trunk rot).

BLACK LOCUST
Robinia pseudoacacia

Look For: For quick identification, look for trees with a rounded to irregular crown, single pinnate, compound leaves and oval-shaped leaflets, strongly fissured furrowed bark, clusters of white flowers in the spring, paired thorns on the stems, and reddish-brown legume pods.

Bark: The trunk is reddish brown to grayish and strongly fissured and furrowed vertically.

Leaves: The leaves are alternate, single pinnately compound, green, 15–35 cm (6–14 inches) long. Each leaf has 9–19 round to oval leaflets that are smooth edged and 2.5–5 cm (1–2 inches) long. Stem spines are usually in pairs and up to 2 cm (0.8 inch) long.

Fruit: Flowers are white and occur in drooping clusters about 15 cm (6 inches) long. The fruit is a legume pod about 5–10 cm (2–4 inches) long and reddish brown (turning brown with age).

Height: Black locust grows to 12–18 m (40–60 feet) and occasionally up to 30+ m (100+ feet) tall. It has trunk diameters of 30–76 cm (12–30 inches) and sometimes up to 1+ m (4+ feet).

Range: Black locust is native to the eastern United States. It has become naturalized throughout most the United States, as well as parts of Canada and Mexico. It occurs throughout Washington, Oregon, California, and southern British Columbia.

Habitat: It is a very invasive tree that spreads into riparian, forest, and grassland communities on the Pacific coast and occurs from 45 to 1,900 m (150–6,200 feet). It is very tolerant of disturbed urban sites.

Associated Species: Common associates include Douglas fir, ponderosa pine, valley oak, California sycamore, black cottonwood, white alder, box elder, and willows.

Similar Trees: Other species with similar leaves include members of the Fabaceae family. Honey locust has similar leaves but they are bipinnate. Acacia has bipinnate compound leaves and the leaflets are normally much smaller.

Tree Risk Hazard Assessment

Biotic and Abiotic Factors: There are a few factors that can cause mortality of black locust, including insects and

Two black locusts in riparian area

Bark

Leaves

Fruit

Spines

Flowers

diseases such as root rot and locust borer. Other signs that indicate that a live tree may have failure potential include one or more conks on the main stem from *Phellinus* sp.

GOODDING OR BLACK WILLOW
Salix gooddingii

Look For: For quick identification for Goodding willow, look for a willow that is a taller tree with an asymmetrical crown without drooping branches, lanceolate to linear leaves that are glabrous and shiny on both surfaces, single scaled buds with an overlapping margin in the back, grayish furrowed bark, growing near streams, and leafless in the winter months.

Bark: The trunk is gray white, thick, vertically fissured, and deeply furrowed.

Leaves: The leaves are alternate, lanceolate, 5–15 cm (2–6 inches) long and wide, green and glabrous on both sides.

Fruit: The flowers are elongate catkins and the fruit is a capsule. The winter bud is single and has overlapping edges.

Height: It commonly grows to 6–18 m (20–60 feet) and up to 30 m (100 feet) tall. It has trunk diameters of 75 cm (30 inches)

Range: Goodding willow occurs in the western United States in west Texas, Nevada, Utah, Colorado, Arizona, New Mexico, and California and northern Mexico. This includes most of California.

Habitat: It grows along streams in riparian forests from 0 to 500 m (0–1,600 feet) in California.

Associated Species: It is commonly associated with trees like sycamore, white alder, Fremont cottonwood, and several other willows (*Salix* spp.).

Similar Trees: Other trees with similar leaf shape are many species of willows. Many willows have hairs or whitish coloring on one or both sides of the leaf. Some other native willow trees are used here for comparison. Red willow has leaves that are white glaucous beneath and is native through much of California and southern Oregon. Peachleaf willow is a tree that is native from east of the Cascade Mountains to the central United States, and its leaves are glaucous beneath. Pacific willow has glaucous leaves underneath, one non-overlapping bud scale, and occurs throughout the West Coast. Mature leaves of Goodding willow are glabrous and shiny on both sides. These four willows mentioned here are probably the tallest native willows on the Pacific coast, and all reach heights of over 12 m (40 feet). Scouler's willow can reach tree

Goodding willow in riparian area

Bark

Female catkin of Goodding willow

Male catkin of Goodding willow

size, has leaf margins revolute on normally obovate leaves, and can occur on riparian or non-riparian sites. Narrowleaf cottonwood has resinous buds with several bud scales.

Tree Risk Hazard Assessment

Biotic and Abiotic Factors: There are a few factors that can cause mortality of black willow, including insects and diseases such as root disease and insect borers. Other signs that indicate a live tree may have high failure potential include excessive stem decay.

Gooding willow leaves in fall

Pacific willow leaves

Peachleaf willow leaves

Young red willow leaves with male and female catkins

REDWOOD
Sequoia sempervirens

Look For: For quick identification, look for trees with a conical crown, thick orange-red brown fibrous bark, green, pointed needles that are flattened along branches, and small cones with thick peltate scales.

Bark: The trunk has thick bark, fibrous, furrowed, and reddish brown, grayish brown in shaded stands.

Needles: The needles are green, pointed, flexible, flattened, 15–25 mm (0.6–1 inch) long. The lower side of the needles are lighter with distinct bands of white stomata.

Cones: Cones are 12–35 mm (0.5–1.5 inches) long, light brown to brown, oblong with thick peltate scales.

Height: It commonly grows to 60 m (200 feet) tall, occasionally up to 115 m (375 feet) tall. It has trunk diameters of 3–4.5 m (10–15 feet) and up to 6 m (20 feet).

Range: Redwood occurs from coastal southwestern Oregon to Southern California coast ranges. This includes the immediate coast and outer coast ranges. It is uncommon in oak woodlands.

Habitat: It grows in mixed evergreen, redwood, and coastal forests from 10 to 975 m (30–3,200 feet).

Associated Species: It is commonly associated with trees like Douglas fir, grand fir, Sitka spruce, bishop pine, Pacific yew, western hemlock, and hardwoods like big-leaf maple, red alder, Pacific madrone, tan oak, California bay, Oregon ash, Oregon white oak, and chinquapin.

Similar Trees: Other conifers with similar needles include grand fir, Pacific yew, and Sitka spruce. Grand fir has longer needles with blunt, notched tips and upright cones. Pacific yew has a flaking thin bark and a berry-like cone. Pacific yew needles appear light dull green glaucous beneath, as opposed to the distinct white stomatal banding of redwood needles underneath. Sitka spruce has very sharp pointed needles, scaly bark, and cones with numerous thin scales. California nutmeg has sharp stiff-pointed needles and different cones. Giant sequoia has similar cones but awl-like short needles.

Tree Risk Hazard Assessment

Biotic and Abiotic Factors: Redwood has resistance to many biotic factors, but armillaria and Phytophthora crown and root rot (*Phytophthora cinnamomi*)

Redwood in redwood forest

Bark

Cones

Needles

can cause tree mortality. Other signs that indicate a live tree may have failure potential include roots rotted from Phytophthora crown and root rot. Dead trees without significant root rot can remain standing for several years.

GIANT SEQUOIA
Sequoiadendron giganteum

Look For: For quick identification, look for trees with a conical crown, thick orange-red brown fibrous bark, short awl-like needles (unique for trees in this book), and small cones with thick peltate scales.

Bark: The trunk has thick bark, fibrous, furrowed, and orange reddish brown.

Needles: The needles are green, awl-like, alternate, 6–12 mm (0.25–0.5 inch) long.

Cones: Cones are 5–8 cm (2–3 inches) long, light brown to brown, oblong with thick peltate scales.

Height: It commonly grows 50–85 m (165–280 feet) tall, occasionally up to 95 m (310 feet) tall. It has trunk diameters up to 6–8 m (20–28 feet).

Range: Giant sequoia occurs in the western Sierra Nevada in California from Placer to Tulare County.

Habitat: It grows in mixed conifer forest at 1,400 to 2,600 m (4,500–8,500 feet).

Associated Species: It is commonly associated with trees like Douglas fir, white fir, sugar pine, ponderosa pine, Jeffrey pine, and black oak.

Similar Trees: Other conifers with awl-like or pointed needles include bristlecone fir, Pacific yew, California nutmeg, and the spruces. Bristlecone fir has longer needles, upright cones, and occurs primarily in the California coast ranges. Pacific yew and California nutmeg have longer needles and a berry- or nutlike fruit. The spruces have longer needles, scaly bark, and cones with numerous thin scales. The cedars, cypresses, and junipers have scalelike needles. Redwood has needles in flattened sprays.

Tree Risk Hazard Assessment

Biotic and Abiotic Factors: Giant sequoia has resistance to many biotic factors, but several root diseases can cause tree mortality, including armillaria, Heterobasidion root disease, and phytophthora root disease. Other signs that indicate a live tree may have failure potential include the same root diseases that can topple these tall trees before death. However, dead trees without extensive root rot can stand for several years.

Giant sequoia with hardwoods in winter months

Bark

Cones

Needles

WESTERN RED CEDAR
Thuja plicata

Look For: For quick identification, look for a conical symmetrical or asymmetrical crown, equal-length leaf scales that are both flat and folded on stem, slightly flattened branches that are distinctly scented, small oblong cones with basal attached scales, and gray to red-brown fibrous bark.

Bark: The trunk on mature trees is gray to reddish brown and fibrous.

Scalelike leaves: The leaf scales are both flat and folded on stem, green, 1.5–6 mm (0.05–0.25 inch) long, and arranged in opposite pairs. The leaf branches are somewhat flattened.

Cones: Cones are light to red brown, 10–20 mm (0.4–0.8 inch) long, oblong when closed, composed of usually 8–12 scales. The cone scales separate and spread upon maturity.

Height: It commonly grows 30–50 m (100–160 feet) tall, occasionally up to 70 m (230 feet) tall. It has trunk diameters of 0.6–1.2 m (2–4 feet), often up to 3 m (10 feet) wide, and can reach 5 m (16 feet) wide.

Range: Western red cedar occurs from southeastern Alaska to western and southern British Columbia, south through Washington and Oregon, to northwestern California. From the Pacific Ocean, it occurs east through northern Idaho to northwestern Montana. This includes coast ranges, Cascades, and northern Rocky Mountains.

Habitat: It grows in coastal, Douglas fir–hemlock–cedar, and true fir (Pacific silver fir) forests at low to medium elevations of 0–2,200 m (0–7,500 feet). It is uncommon in subalpine forests.

Associated Species: It is commonly associated with trees like Sitka spruce, western hemlock, Pacific silver fir, Alaska yellow cedar, grand fir, western larch, lodgepole pine, incense cedar, Port Orford cedar (southern part of range), hardwoods like red alder, bigleaf maple, and black cottonwood.

Similar Trees: Other cedars, cypresses, and junipers can all appear similar due to their scalelike needles. Juniper trees have berry cones, have rounded branches, and occur in drier habitats. The cypresses of California have round cones, have rounded branches, and occur in drier habitats. Alaska yellow cedar has more of a whitish gray bark, more drooping branches, different-type cones with peltate scales, and usually occur at higher

Western red cedar in riparian area

Bark

elevations. Incense cedar has more flattened branches and alternating leaf scale lengths. Port Orford cedar has cones with peltate scales, and the underside of the branches have more pronounced X-shaped lines of white stomata. Crushed needles of western red cedar have a distinct scent that differs from that of other cedars and other conifers.

Cone and scalelike leaves

Tree Risk Hazard Assessment

Biotic and Abiotic Factors: Few insects and diseases can contribute to western red cedar mortality including armillaria and cedar bark beetle (*Phloeosinus sequoia*). Other signs that indicate that a live tree may have failure potential include trunk rot. Western red cedars are easily windthrown in waterlogged soils. It is normal to see dead tops on living western red cedar.

WESTERN HEMLOCK
Tsuga heterophylla

Look For: For quick identification, look for a narrow conical symmetrical crown, short, usually flattened needles of differing lengths and stomata on the lower surfaces, small short cones, and gray bark shallowly furrowed in vertical-shaped plates and ridges.

Bark: The trunk on mature trees is gray, furrowed in vertical ridges.

Needles: The needles are green above with bands of white stomata below, appearing flattened, 5–20 mm (0.2–0.8 inch) long.

Cones: The cone is pendant, red brown, 15–30 mm (0.6–1.2 inches) long.

Height: It commonly grows 50–60 m (160–200 feet) tall, occasionally up to 80 m (260 feet) tall. It has trunk diameters of 0.6–1.2 m (2–4 feet), occasionally up to 3 m (9 feet) wide.

Range: Western hemlock occurs from southern Alaska, through western and southern British Columbia, south through Washington and Oregon, to northwestern California. From the Pacific Ocean, it occurs east through northern Idaho to northwestern Montana. This includes coast ranges, Cascades, and northern Rocky Mountains.

Habitat: It grows in Douglas fir–hemlock–cedar, coastal, true fir forests at low to medium elevations of 0–1,650 m (0–5,500 feet). It is uncommon in subalpine forests.

Associated Species: It is commonly associated with trees like Douglas fir, Sitka spruce, western red cedar, Pacific silver fir, Alaska yellow cedar, grand fir, western larch, lodgepole pine, Port Orford cedar (southern part of range), redwood (southern part of range), mountain hemlock (northern part of range), hardwoods like red alder, and big-leaf maple.

Similar Trees: Other trees with similar needles include mountain hemlock, Douglas fir and spruces. Mountain hemlock has spiraled needles as opposed to flattened in western hemlock, and mountain hemlock cones are longer. Douglas fir and the spruces have longer needles that are spirally attached. Spruces have scaly bark with usually stiff point needles. Douglas fir has cones with exserted bracts. Needles of western and mountain hemlock have a distinct scent that differs from that of other conifers.

Western hemlock in Douglas fir–hemlock–cedar forest

Bark

Cone and needles

Tree Risk Hazard Assessment

Biotic and Abiotic Factors: There are several factors that can cause mortality of western hemlock, including insects and diseases such as armillaria root rot, annosus root disease, laminated root disease, western hemlock looper, green-striped forest looper, western black-headed budworm, dwarf mistletoe (*Arceuthobium tsugense* ssp. *tsugense*), and web blight (*Rhizoctonia butunii*). Other signs that indicate that a live tree may have high failure potential include one or more conks on the main stem (Indian paint fungus).

Cone and needles

MOUNTAIN HEMLOCK
Tsuga mertensiana

Look For: For quick identification, look for a narrow conical symmetrical crown with a straight or drooping tip, spirally arranged short needles with white stomata on both surfaces, medium-length narrow cones, and gray bark furrowed in irregular or diagonal-shaped plates and ridges.

Bark: The trunk on mature trees is gray, furrowed in diagonal irregular plates.

Needles: The needles are blue green, spiraled around the branches, 10–25 mm (0.35–1 inch) long, stiff.

Cones: The cone is pendant, red brown, 3–8 cm (1–3 inches) long.

Height: It commonly grows from 20 to 40 m (66–130 feet) tall, occasionally up to 60 m (195 feet) tall. It has trunk diameters of 0.8–1 m (2.5–3.5 feet), occasionally up to 2 m (6.5 feet) wide.

Range: Mountain hemlock occurs from south-central Alaska to western and southern British Columbia, south through Washington and Oregon, to the southern Sierra Nevada of California. It also occurs from the Pacific Ocean east through northern Idaho to northwestern Montana. This includes coast ranges, Klamath Mountains, Cascades, and northern Rocky Mountains.

Habitat: It grows in a diversity of habitats including coastal (southeastern Alaska), true fir, subalpine forests, and subboreal white spruce hardwood, at low to high elevations from 0 to 1,000 m (0–3,300 feet) in the northern part of its range and 2,500–3,500 m (8,200–11,400 feet) in the southern part of its range.

Associated Species: It is commonly associated with trees like Sitka spruce (southern Alaska), western hemlock, Pacific silver fir, Alaska yellow cedar, noble fir, Engelmann spruce, white fir, lodgepole pine, whitebark pine, white spruce (in southern Alaska), western white pine, limber pine, Jeffrey pine, and red and Shasta fir.

Similar Trees: Other trees with similar needles include western hemlock, Douglas fir, and spruces. Western hemlock has flattened needles as opposed to spirally arranged in mountain hemlock, and western hemlock cones are shorter. Douglas fir and the spruces have longer needles. Spruces have scaly bark with usually stiff-point needles. Douglas fir has cones with exserted bracts. Needles of mountain and western hemlock have a distinct scent that differs from that of other conifers.

Bark

Mountain hemlock in true fir forest

Cone and needles

Tree Risk Hazard Assessment

Biotic and Abiotic Factors: There are several factors that can cause mortality of mountain hemlock, including diseases such as annosus root disease, laminated root disease, dwarf mistletoe (*A. tsugense* ssp. *mertensianae*). Other signs that indicate that a live tree may have high failure potential include one or more conks on the main stem (Indian paint fungus).

Cone and needles

SIBERIAN ELM
Ulmus pumila

Look For: For quick identification, look for trees with a rounded crown, single, alternate, serrated leaves, strongly furrowed and ridged bark, circular fruits that are winged all around, and globular leaf buds with white hairy scale margins.
Bark: The trunk is grayish brown and strongly furrowed and vertically ridged.
Leaves: Leaves are green, simple, serrated, alternate, lanceolate-elliptic, deciduous, 3–8 cm (1.5–3 inches) long.
Fruit: The fruit is rounded samara, about 1 cm (0.3 inch), and winged all around.
Height: Siberian elm grows 15–20 m (50–70 feet) tall and sometimes up to 25 m (85 feet) tall. It has trunk diameters of up to 1 m (3.5 feet).
Range: Siberian elm is native to central and eastern Asia. It has become naturalized throughout most of the United States except the Southeast. It occurs throughout Washington, Oregon, and California.
Habitat: It is a very invasive tree that spreads into riparian areas, pastures and rangelands, and disturbed right of ways from 20 to 1,500 m (65–5,000 feet).
Associated Species: Other riparian trees like cottonwoods and willows when it is growing in riparian areas.
Similar Trees: Other species with similar leaves include other landscaping elms with similar bark features. Those elm trees usually have pointed buds and larger leaves. American elm usually has pointed buds, and the bud scale margins are normally not long white hairy. Alders and paper birch have larger leaves and a different type of fruit. Cherry (*Prunus* spp.) trees usually have a smoother lenticelled bark and a different type of fruit.

Tree Risk Hazard Assessment
Biotic and Abiotic Factors: Literature states very little about abiotic and biotic factors causing tree mortality for Siberian elm. Root rot can cause mortality. Siberian elm is not very susceptible to Dutch elm disease, but American elm is. There are American elms that have succumbed to Dutch elm disease in California. Other signs that indicate a live tree may have failure potential include decay from stem cankers.

Siberian elm in pasture

Bark

Fruit

Leaves

CALIFORNIA BAY
Umbellularia californica

Look For: For quick identification, look for a tree with a rounded to spreading crown that has alternate, evergreen leaves with smooth margins and a purple-colored fruit at maturity. The leaves are very strongly scented. Bark on mature trees is irregularly cracked or furrowed and usually with a distinct pattern.

Bark: The trunk is grayish with irregular vertical cracking and also can become slightly furrowed.

Leaves: The leaves are shiny dark green on top and bottom, alternate, evergreen, lanceolate to oblong, 3–10 cm (2–4 inches) long, smooth edged, and strongly scented.

Fruit: The fruit is berry-like or nutlike, green turning purple at maturity, 20–25 mm (0.8–1 inch) long.

Height: It commonly grows to 12–24 m (40–80 feet) and occasionally up to 30 m (100 feet) tall. It has trunk diameters of 45–75 cm (18–30 inches) and up to 2 m (6 feet).

Range: California bay occurs from southwestern Oregon south through the California coast ranges to the Southern California mountains. It also occurs in the Sierra Nevada.

Habitat: It grows in mixed evergreen, chaparral, oak woodlands, and riparian and redwood forests from 0 to 1,500 m (0–5,000 feet).

Associated Species: It is commonly associated with many different trees throughout its range including hardwoods like canyon live oak, coast live oak, black cottonwood, willows, sycamore, big-leaf maple, tan oak, Pacific madrone, box elder, red alder, valley oak, *Eucalyptus* spp., and conifers like redwood, Coulter pine, big-cone Douglas fir, Douglas fir, and Port Orford cedar.

Similar Trees: Other trees with similar leaves are Shreve oak and interior live oak. Shreve oak and interior live oak have smooth or toothed leaf margins, visible veins on the leaves, and an acorn for a fruit. Pacific madrone has more-ovate leaves with a completely different trunk that is reddish.

Tree Risk Hazard Assessment

Biotic and Abiotic Factors: California bay has resistance to many biotic factors, nothing serious for mature tree mortality. A sign that indicates a live tree may have high failure potential include one or more conks on the main stem (*Ganoderma brownii*).

Two California bay trees in mixed evergreen forest

Fruit and leaves

Fruit and leaves

Bark

MEXICAN FAN PALM
Washingtonia robusta

Look For: For quick identification, look for a palm that can grow to 100 feet tall, palmate fronds, bulbous tree base, clusters of small black-berried fruits, has a thin and flexible trunk, and occurs in areas with hot summers and/or mild winters.

Bark: When the old fronds and their bases are removed, the trunk is light brown turning gray with age, from a swollen base, with small horizontal ridges and vertical striations.

Leaves: The fronds consist of green leaves and spined petioles up to 2 m (6.5 feet) long. The fronds are palmate, in a compact crown, and the inflorescences are up to 3 m (10 feet) long.

Fruit: The flowers are orange pink, and the fruit is a spherical blue-black drupe and 6–10 mm (0.24–0.4 in) long.

Height: Mexican fan palm commonly grows to 25 m (80 feet) tall, occasionally up to 30 m (100 feet) tall. It has trunk diameters of 30–80 cm (1–2.5 feet) wide.

Range: Mexican fan palm is native to northwestern Mexico. It has become naturalized and is used for landscaping in California and several other states in the southern United States. Mexican fan palm is the focus of palms, since it is the tallest and most likely to cause damage to power lines and other objects.

Habitat: It can spread into riparian areas and other locations that do not fall below 18 degrees Fahrenheit. It usually becomes more easily naturalized in the southern half of California under more ideal growing temperatures.

Associated Species: Commonly landscaping trees, and can occur with cottonwoods, sycamore, and willows when in riparian areas.

Similar Trees: California fan palm (*Washingtonia filifera*) is the only native palm in California and has a limited native range in the Colorado desert area of southeastern California. It is most similar to Mexican fan palm, but it usually does not have an abruptly swollen base, has a thicker trunk, smaller and less spines on the frond petiole, and is shorter at maturity. The cultivated hybrid between California and Mexican fan palm is a popular landscaping tree and makes identification more difficult. Canary

native range
planted range

Planted range in United States and native range in Mexico

Mexican fan palm in riparian area

Lower trunk

Fruit

Island date palm is popular for landscaping and is also becoming naturalized in California, but that palm has pinnate leaf fronds.

Tree Risk Hazard Assessment

Biotic and Abiotic Factors: There are several factors that can cause mortality of Mexican fan palm, including insects and diseases such as Ganoderma butt rot, Thielaviopsis and Phytophthora bud rot, Fusarium wilt, and palm borers (*Dinapate wrightii*). Other signs that indicate that a live tree may have high failure potential include signs of palm borer. A live palm can bend and strike power lines during high-wind storms. Falling dead fronds and inflorescences are an additional hazard to power lines and objects below during high winds.

Leaf frond

BIBLIOGRAPHY

Angwin, P. A., et al. *Hazard Tree Guidelines for Forest Service Facilities and Roads in the Pacific Southwest Region*. [Online]. Forest Health Protection Pacific Southwest Region April 2012 (Report # RO-12-01). Available: www.fs.usda .gov/Internet/FSE_DOCUMENTS/stelprdb5332560.pdf.

Baldwin, B., et al. (eds.). 2012. *The Jepson Manual*: *Vascular Plants of California*. University of California Press.

Baldwin, K., et al. 2020. "Vegetation Zones of Canada: A Biogeoclimatic Perspective." Natural Resources Canada. Sault Ste. Marie, Ontario, Canada. Also available online: www.nrcan.gc.ca/forests/research-centres/glfc/13459.

Bark & Wood Boring Beetles. 2019 [Online]. California Forest Pest Council. Available: www.caforestpestcouncil.org/bark-beetles.

Behrmann, B. N., and R. Oliver. 2021. "Invasive Shothole Borers: An Ongoing Threat to California's Trees." *Western Arborist*.

Bliss, L. C., et al. 2010. Vegetation Regions. [Online]. *The Canada Encyclopedia*. Available: www.thecanadianencyclopedia.ca/en/article/ vegetation-regions.

Boyd, V. 2022. "Death by a Thousand Cankers." [Online]. *West Coast Nut*. JCS, Marketing Inc. Available: www.wcngg.com/2022/04/18/death-by-a-thousand-cankers.

Braatne, J. H., et al. 2006. "Naturalization of Plains Cottonwood (*Populus Deltoides* Subsp. *Monilifera*) along River Drainages West of the Rocky Mountains." *Western North American Naturalist* 66, pp. 310–32.

British Columbia Forestry. [Online]. Available: www2.gov.bc.ca/gov/content/ industry/.

Broschat, T. K. 1993. *Washingtonia robusta*: Mexican Fan Palm. UF IFAS Extension, University of Florida. ENH-827.

Burke Herbarium Image Collection. Vascular Plants, Macrofungi, & Lichenized Fungi of Washington. [Online]. Burke Museum Herbarium, University of Washington, Seattle. Available: https://burkeherbarium.org/ imagecollection/.

Burleigh, J., T. Ebata, K. J. White, D. Rusch, and H. Kope (eds.). 2014. *Field Guide to Forest Damage in British Columbia* (Joint publication, ISSN 0843-4719; no. 17).

Calflora. [Online]. Calflora, Berkely, CA. www.calflora.org.

California Forest Insect and Disease Training Manual. [Online]. US Forest Service, Region 5, Forest Health Protection and the California Department of Forestry and Fire Protection, Forest Pest Management forest health specialists. Available: www.fs.usda.gov/Internet/FSE_DOCUMENTS/ fsbdev3_046410.pdf.

Callan, B. B. *Diseases of* Populus *in British Columbia: A Diagnostic Manual.* Natural Resources Canada. Canadian Forest Service.

Costello, L. R., et al. 2003. *Abiotic Disorders of Landscape Plants: A Diagnostic Guide.* University of California Agriculture and Natural Resources. Publication 3420.

Costello, L. R., et al. 2011. *Oaks in the Urban Landscape: Selection, Care, and Preservation.* University of California.

DeVelice, R. L., et al. 1999. *Plant Community Types of the Chugach National Forest: Southcentral Alaska.* United States Department of Agriculture Forest Service Chugach National Forest Alaska Region. Technical Publication. RT10-TP-76.

Dunster, J. A. 2017. *Tree Risk Assessment Manual*, Second Edition. International Society of Arboriculture.

Earle, C. J. The Gymnosperm Database. [Online]. Available: www.conifers.org.

Edmonds, R. L., et al. 2011. *Forest Health and Protection.* Waveland Press Inc.

E-Flora BC: Electronic Atlas of the Flora of British Columbia. [Online]. Available: www.//ibis.geog.ubc.ca/biodiversity/eflora/.

Elliot, M. [Online]. 2018. Bud Rot of Palm. UFI/IFAS Extension. University of Florida. Publication 220. Available: PP-220/PP144: Bud Rot of Palm (ufl .edu). www.edis.ifas.ufl.edu/publication/PP144.

Filip, G. M. *Field Guide for Hazard-Tree Identification and Mitigation on Developed Sites in Oregon and Washington Forests.* 2014. [Online]. R6-NR-TP-021-2013 USDA Forest Service, Forest Health Protection, Pacific Northwest Region, Portland, OR. Available: www.fs.usda.gov/Internet/ FSE_DOCUMENTS/stelprd3799993.pdf.

Fire Effects Information System. [Online]. US Department of Agriculture, Forest Service, Rocky Mountain Research Station, Missoula Fire Sciences Laboratory (Producer). Available: www.feis-crs.org/feis/.

Flora of North America. [Online]. Available: www.efloras.org.

Forest and Insect Disease Leaflets (FIDLs). [Online]. USDA Forest Service. United States Department of Agriculture. Available: FIDLs (usda.gov). www.fs.usda.gov/foresthealth/publications/fidls/index.shtml.

Franklin, J. F., and C. T. Dyrness. 1973. *Natural Vegetation of Oregon and Washington.* Pacific Northwest Forest and Range Experiment Station Forest Service, US Department of Agriculture, Portland, Oregon. USDA Forest Service General Technical Report PNW-8.

Goheen, E. M., and E. A. Willhite. 2006. *Field Guide to the Common Diseases and Insect Pests of Oregon and Washington Conifers.* R6-NR-FID-PR-01-06. Portland, OR. USDA Forest Service, Pacific Northwest Region.

Hadfield, J. S., et al. [Online]. *Root Diseases of Oregon and Washington Conifers.* US Department of Agriculture, Forest Service, Pacific Northwest Region, Forest Pest Management, Portland, Oregon. Available: www.fs.usda.gov/detail/r6/forest-grasslandhealth/insects-diseases/?cid=fsbdev2_027376.

Hagen, B. W. 2020. "Destructive Pests and Pathogens of California's Native Oaks." *Western Arborist.*

Hatch, C. R. 2007. *Trees of the California Landscape.* University of California Press.

Hishinuma, S., et al. 2011. *Goldspotted Oak Borer Field Identification Guide.* University of California. Agricultural and Natural Resources.

Insects and Diseases. [Online]. US Forest Service. Caring for the Land and Serving People. Pacific Northwest Region. Available: Region 6—Insects & Diseases (usda.gov). www.fs.usda.gov/detail/r6/forest-grasslandhealth/insects-diseases.

Intermountain Region Herbarium Network. [Online]. Available: Consortium of Intermountain Herbaria Collection Search Parameters. www.intermountainbiota.org/portal/collections/harvestparams.php.

Katovich, S. L., et al. "Bronze birch borer." *Forest Insect & Disease Leaflet 111.* US Department of Agriculture.

Lillybridge, T. R., et al. October 1995. *Field Guide for Forested Plant Associations of the Wenatchee National Forest.* US Department of Agriculture Forest Service Pacific Northwest Research Station General Technical Report PNW-GTR-359.

Little, Elbert L., Jr. 1966–1978. [Online]. US Department of Agriculture, Forest Service, and others—USGS Geosciences and Environmental Change Science Center: Digital Representations of Tree Species Range Maps from *Atlas of United States Trees* (and other publications). www.usgs.gov/centers/geosciences-and-environmental-change-science-center.

Lloyd, J. 1997. *Plant Health Care for Woody Ornamentals. A Professional's Guide to Preventing and Managing Environmental Stresses and Pests.* International Society of Arboriculture.

McCreary, D., and G. Nadar. January 2011. Publication 8445. *Burned Oaks: Which Ones Will Survive?* University of California Agricultural and Natural Resource.

Meidinger, D., and J. Pojar. 1991. *Ecosystems of British Columbia.* BC Ministry of Forests.

Moore, D. 2014. *Trees of Arkansas.* Arkansas Forestry Commission.

Mulvey, R. T., et al. 2013. "Swiss Needle Cast." *Forest Insect & Disease Leaflet 181.* US Department of Agriculture. Forest Service.

National Atlas. 1966. Potential Natural Vegetation. US Department of the Interior, Geological Service, Reston VA.

National Atlas. 1967. Major Forest Types. US Geological Survey, Denver, CO.

Natural Resources Canada: Trees. [Online]. Available: https://tidcf.nrcan.gc.ca/en/trees.

NatureServe Explorer. [Online]. Available: https://explorer.natureserve.org.

Oester, P. T., et al. 2018. *Managing Insects and Diseases of Oregon Conifers.* Oregon State University Extension Service. EM 8980.

One Earth. [Online]. Available: www.oneearth.org.

Oregon Flora. [Online]. OSU, Corvallis, OR. Available: www.oregonflora.org.

Owen, D. R., et al. April 2015. Number 33. *Survival of Fire-Injured Conifers in California.* California Department of Forestry and Fire Protection.

Pacific Northwest Pest Management Handbooks. [Online]. Available: https://pnwhandbooks.org.

Pelt, R. V. [Online]. *Identifying Mature and Old Forests in Washington.* Washington State Department of Natural Resources. Hilary S. Franz. Commissioner of Public Lands. Available: Identifying Mature and Old Forests in Washington | WA—DNR. www.dnr.wa.gov/programs-and-services/forest-resources/habitat-conservation/identifying-mature-and-old-forests.

Sawyer, J. O., et al. 2008. *A Manual of California Vegetation.* California Native Plant Society Press.

SelecTree. [Online]. Available: SelecTree: A Tree Selection Guide. https://selectree.calpoly.edu.

SFGate. [Online]. Available: www.sfgate.com.

Shive, K., and S. Kocher. July 2017. ANR Publication 8386. *Recovering from Wildfire: A Guide for California's Land Forest Owners.* University of California Agricultural and Natural Resources.

Simpson, M. July 2007. *Forested Plant Associations of the Oregon East Cascades.* United States Department of Agriculture Forest Service Pacific Northwest Region Technical Paper R6-NR-ECOL-TP-03-2007.

Southern Research station. [Online]. USDA, US Forest Service. Asheville, NC. Available: www.srs.fs.usda.gov.

Stem Decays. [Online]. Available: https://apps.fs.usda.gov/r6_decaid/views/stem_decay.html.

Svihra, P., and C. S. Koehler. 1993. "Flatheaded Borer in White Alder Landscape Trees." *Journal of Arboriculture* 19 (5), pp. 260–265.

Swiecki, T. J., and E. A. Bernhardt. 2006. *A Field Guide to Insects and Diseases of California Oaks*. United States Department of Agriculture Forest Service Pacific Southwest Research Station General Technical Report PSW-GTR-197.

Toupin, R., et al. 2008. *Field Guide for Danger Tree Identification and Response*. United States Department of Agriculture Forest Service Pacific Northwest Region. United States Department of Interior Bureau of Land Management. R6-NR-FP-PR-01-08.

UC IPM. [Online]. State Integrated Pest Management Program. University of California Agricultural & Natural Resources. Available: UC Statewide IPM Program. http://ipm.ucanr.edu.

USDA. [Online]. Animal and Plant Health Inspection Service. US Department of Agriculture. Available: USDA APHIS | www.aphis.usda.gov/aphis/home/.

US Fish & Wildlife Service. Whitebark pine receives ESA protection as a threatened species—Significant threats continue to challenge this keystone species of the American West. 2022. [Online]. https://www.fws.gov/press-release/2022-12/whitebark-pine-receives-esa-protection-threatened-species.

Wagener, W. W. 1963. *Judging Hazard from Native Trees in California Recreational Areas: A Guide for Professional Foresters*. Pacific Southwest Forest and Range Experiment Station—Berkeley, California Forest Service—U. S. Department of Agriculture. US Forest Service Research Paper PSW-P1.

Westfall, J., and M. D. Holt. 2021. *2021 Summary of Forest Health Conditions in British Columbia*. British Columbia. Ministry of Forests, Lands, Natural Resource Operations and Rural Development. Pest Management Report Number 15. Available: aer_ov_2021 (1).pdf.

Wikipedia. [Online]. Available: Wikipedia, the free encyclopedia www.wikipedia.org.

Williams, C. K., and T. R. Lillybridge. 1983. *Forested Plant Associations of the Okanogan National Forest*. United States Department of Agriculture. Forest Service. Pacific Northwest Region. R6-Ecol-132b.

Williams, C. K., et al. 1995. *Forested Plant Associations of the Colville National Forest*. United States Department of Agriculture. Forest Service. Pacific Northwest Research Station. General Technical Report PNW GTR-360.

Wood, D. L., et al. 2003. *Pests of the California Conifers.* University of California Press. www.ucpress.edu/ebook/9780520936379/pests-of-the-native-california-conifers.

GLOSSARY

acorn. Usually one seed encoded in a hard shell with a cap attached, like in Quercus.

acuminate. In a leaf, long tapered pointed tip.

acute. In a leaf, leaf sides at the tip converging at less than 90 degrees.

allelopathy. Chemical compounds produced in plants that can inhibit other plants or animal species.

berry. A fleshy fruit with one or more seeds that are not encased in a hard stonelike center, like a drupe is.

bipinnate. A compound leaf in which each leaflet is pinnately compound (e.g., *Acacia dealbata*).

brown rot. Heartwood and sapwood decay involving breakdown of cellulose, leaving a hard crumbly wood.

buds. Located at the tips or along a branch where new leaves are developed.

canker. Decay originating from sapwood or heartwood, usually visible on stem surface with swelling.

capsule. A dry fruit of two or more valves that usually splits by pores or slits.

catkin. Tight clusters of male or female flowers on elongated pendant spikes. Salix has male and female catkins.

chambered pith. After cutting a small branch lengthwise, an interior with square or rectangular chambers is present (e.g., walnut trees).

chaparral. Habitats dominated by evergreen shrubs like chamise (*Adenostoma* spp.), shrubby oaks (*Quercus* spp.), Ceanothus (*Ceanothus* spp.), Manzanita (*Arctostaphylos*), sage (*Salvia* spp.), normally adapted to fire. California chaparral occurs in southwestern Oregon, California, and Baja California in Mexico.

climax. Tree species that perpetuate in time in a forest stand without disturbances like fires, windstorms, logging, etc.

compound leaf. Leaf divided into several leaflets, usually with a stem attached to the leaflets.

cone. Referring to female seed-bearing structure of gymnosperms.

conk. Reproductive structure of a fungus that appears like a shelf, usually on the main stems of trees.

cordate. Referring to a leaf that is somewhat heart-shaped.

crenate. Referring to the edge of a leaf with shallow rounded teeth.

deciduous. Usually referring to leaves that grow and fall in the same year.

decurrent. When referring to tree form, usually several branches arising from main stem with a spreading shaped crown, often a hardwood tree.

doubly serrate. Referring to the edge of a leaf when the serrations all have smaller teeth on their edges.

drupe. Fleshy fruit with a skin on the outside and a hard seed in the center.

edaphic. Referring to a soil being influenced by drainage (i.e., wet soils) or texture (e.g., rocky soils) conditions.

epicormic branches. Branches usually originating from wounds or pruning operations above the base of the tree. Can have the potential to fail.

excurrent. When referring to tree form, usually one main stem with a pyramidal or cone-shaped crown, often a conifer tree.

fascicle. Referring to needles of the genus Pinus that are bundled or grouped and enclosed in a sheath of one to five needles.

fruit. Referring to female seed-bearing structure of angiosperms.

fungal hyphae. Vegetative part of fungus, usually as threadlike filaments.

glaucous. Surfaces are covered or appear to be covered with a whitish waxy or powdery film.

leaf bud scar. Usually below a leaf bud, location where previous leaf has dropped.

leaf buds. Buds attached to the stem can have one or multiple scales, useful in winter identification after leaves have fallen.

leaf or scale gland. Small pit in the leaf scale of a tree in the Cupressaceae family, with or without resin.

leaf or scale resin. Usually refers to a drop of clear resin in the gland of a leaf scale in the Cupressaceae family.

legume. A dry to fleshy pod with two valves containing one or more seeds.

lenticel. Spongy or callused areas of different sizes, shapes, and colors; usually on the bark of trees or shrubs (e.g., Prunus).

Level 1 assessment. Limited visual assessment that can be performed by walking, driving by the trees in a vehicle, or flying by the trees in aircraft.

Level 2 assessment. Basic assessment involving walking around the tree and inspecting it from crown to base of tree from the ground.

Level 3 assessment. Advanced assessment of the tree that can involve one or several of the following: climbing the tree for crown inspections, assessment for stem decay with mechanical or electronic equipment, performing load tests, and root excavations.

mesic. Referring to a forest habitat with a well-balanced supply of moisture.

montane. Referring to a forest community below subalpine in elevation.

needle. Synonym for leaf of the species in the Pinaceae family, Taxaceae family, and a few species in the Cupressaceae family.

nut. Fruit enclosed in a hard shell, considered an acorn when it had a cap.

obovate. Usually referring to a leaf that is wider above the middle toward the tip than at the base.

obtuse. In a leaf, leaf sides converging at greater than 90 degrees.

palmate. Several leaves attached at one point. Palmate leaf lobing appears to originate from one point (e.g., species of Acer).

peltate scale. Scale on a conifer cone that is centrally attached.

phloem. Transports carbohydrates through the tree.

pine needle fascicle. Pine needles grouped in clusters of one to five, wrapped in a sheath at the base of the needles.

pinnate leaves. Leaves with more than one leaflet on a common petiole, but arising from the same bud. Leaflets attached at different points on a stem. Pinnate leaf lobing appears to originate at different points of a leaf midvein (e.g., species of Quercus).

pome. Fleshy fruit where the hard seeds are partially enclosed by papery walled segments.

poor soil. A soil that lacks high levels of nutrients like nitrogen, phosphorus, and potassium and is not ideal for growing large healthy trees.

pure stands. When one tree species occupies nearly 100 percent of the area.

revolute or recurved. A curving back of a structure like a leaf edge.

samara fruit. Winged achene, a one-seeded fruit with a wing attached.

scale. Synonym for leaf of many species in the Cupressaceae family and the genus Tamarix. Also buds of conifers and hardwoods can consist of one or more scales (e.g., Salix species have a bud with one scale).

semi-deciduous. Referring to leaves that fall and are replaced by new ones, possibly biannually or during extreme climatic conditions.

seral. Tree species that pioneer or initiate in forest stands with disturbances like fires, windstorms, logging, etc.

serpentine soil. Considered a poor soil with higher concentrations of metals like nickel, iron, chromium, and cobalt. Fewer species of plants grow on soils like this.

serrate. Referring to the edge of a leaf with sharp, fine to coarse teeth.

serrulate. Finer and smaller teeth than in serrate.

sign. Physical evidence of an abiotic or biotic causal agent (e.g., larval galleries under the bark of a tree is sign of bark beetles).

simple leaves. Leaves with one leaflet on a petiole, arising from a bud.

soil edaphic. Soil characteristics like type of nutrients, acidity, water content, and aeration.

stellate hairs. Numerous hair points projecting from one similar basal point.

stomata, white. Usually occurring in white bands on conifers needles or scales.

symptom. A plant's reaction to a disorder from an abiotic or biotic causal agent (e.g., dead foliage can be a symptom of many different abiotic and biotic agents).

tomentose. Thick covering of hairs.

tridentine or forked bracts. Three forked bracts exserted beneath cone scales of Douglas fir.

true firs. Trees in the genus Abies with upright female cones that break apart at maturity.

urn-shaped. Referring to a flower that is widened at the base and narrowing to the tip.

white rot. Heartwood and sapwood decay involving breakdown of lignin, leaving spongy wood.

whorled leaves. Several leaves or leaflets arising from same point or node on the petiole.

xylem. Transports water and nutrients throughout the tree.

ABOUT THE AUTHOR

Robert Weiss is a career botanist, ISA Board-Certified Master Arborist, and holds a master's of science degree in Forest Ecology. He designed and developed this book while working as an arborist on various vegetation projects, subcontracting for Southern California Edison in California. The contents of this book were inspired in part by the job duties on these various projects.

Weiss performed an extensive literature review and sought help from reviewers to complete the abiotic and biotic causes of tree mortality and live-tree failure portions of this book. While some of the abiotic and biotic causes of tree mortality and failure of mature trees are included, the tables *are not* all-inclusive but cover the basics of biotic and abiotic factors. More information on biotic and abiotic issues can be obtained from the resources in the bibliography or consulting with a local or regional professional in their respective fields. He would encourage readers of this book to learn and use the taxonomic keys along with the written descriptions and photos. Use of the taxonomic keys can greatly increase overall accuracy of tree identification.